DATE DUE

JUN 1 2 2000	

DEMCO

Additional praise for

тhe ɡendeſed дtom

"An ambitious, lively, learned, and highly readable riff on *Frankenstein* that ranges from Romantic theory to postmodern physics in its quest to investigate the (en)gendering of what Mary Shelley's mad scientist calls his 'hideous progeny.'" — Sandra M. Gilbert, Professor of English, University of California at Davis, author of *No Man's Land: The Place of the Woman Writer in the Twentieth Century* and coauthor of *Mad Woman in the Attic: The Woman Writer and the Nineteenth Century Literary Imagination*

"In a voice both personal and scholarly, witty and literate, Theodore Roszak adds his analysis to the feminist critique of masculinist science. This work traces atomistic thought in science through the multiple perspectives of history, literature, and feminist psychology. Roszak demonstrates quite convincingly — through the use of the Frankenstein myth, the life events of Mary Shelley, and a careful application of feminist psychology — that the concept of the minute atom carries all the cultural weight of the gendered vision that has come close to destroying nature itself. Roszak joins forces, in this work, with those who have successfully uncloaked the objective garb of modern science to expose the masculine body of knowledge beneath it. *The Gendered Atom* adds significantly to a distinguished career of fine scholarship and passionate social criticism." — Ellyn Kaschak, Professor of Psychology, San Jose State University, author of *Engendered Lives: A New Psychology of Women's Experience*; coeditor, *Women and Therapy*

"A provocative and well-written view of problems in science and the psychology of gender." — Evelyn Fox Keller, Professor of the History and Philosophy of Science, Massachusetts Institute of Technology, author of *Reflections on Gender and Science*

The Gendered Atom

Reflections on the sexual psychology of science

 Theodore Roszak

Foreword by
Jane Goodall

CONARI PRESS
Berkeley, California

Copyright © 1999 by Theodore Roszak

Conari Press books are distributed by Publishers Group West.
Jacket and book design: Claudia Smelser
Cover photograph: Courtesy of Photodisc

Library of Congress Cataloging-in-Publication Data

Roszak, Theodore
    The gendered atom : reflections on the sexual psychology of science / Theodore Roszak : foreword by Jane Goodall.
        p.   cm.
    Includes bibliographical references.
    ISBN: 1-57324-171-7 (hardcover)
    1. Science and psychology. 2. Psychology—Philosophy.
    3. Sex (Psychology) 4. Feminist psychology. I. Title.
BF64.R69   1999   99–16074
501—dc21   CIP

Printed in the United States of America on recycled paper.

99 00 01 02 DATA 10 9 8 7 6 5 4 3 2 1

For Betty,
With Betty

table of contents

Foreword by Jane Goodall   ix

1 Frankenstein, Feminism, and the Fate of the Earth   1

2 The Nuclear Winter of 1816   23

3 The Largest Scientific Machine in the World   29

4 The Psychology of the Quark   45

5 "The Power Is There"   63

6 Macho Science   73

7 The Rape of Nature   93

8 "The Corpse of My Dead Mother. . ."   109

9 Deep Community   119

10 The Black Madonna   135

11 "Only Connect!"   143

Afterword: The Idols of the Bedchamber   153

Notes   157

Bibliography   167

About the Author   175

foreword

by Jane Goodall

The Gendered Atom is a challenging book. And it is an important book, in that it poses questions and raises issues that Western scientists seldom consider and with which they are ill equipped to deal. Scientists, striving to understand the world in which we live, are taught to value objectivity above all. Yet, as Theodore Roszak points out, we cannot remove ourselves from the equation. However much we, as scientists, may try to be impersonal objective observers, we cannot escape our individuality; we bring our own values and ideas to our work. These ideas reflect our culture, our family backgrounds, the times in which we live, and, as Roszak believes, our gender. Only when we admit to this will we realize the extent to which we may unintentionally bias our interpretations of our observations, or the very nature of the questions we ask.

Western science, until recently the domain of men, has long held an overly simplistic, mechanistic view of our world. For example, scientists have typically asserted that animals are little more than machines, incapable of feeling pain or any human-like emotions. However complex a behavioral interaction seemed to be, the most parsimonious, the simplest explanation was considered the most scientific—and therefore the best. More recently, the field of sociobiology has contributed to scientific reductionism. These attitudes, compounded by increasing urbanization along with our selfish, materialistic lifestyles, have led to a gradual alienation from the natural world. We have cut ourselves off from our roots. Whereas indigenous people see themselves as part of nature and live in harmony with a world in which other animals are their brothers and sisters, many scientists (and other people) today believe that we are part of a great unfeeling machine in which animals are considered lower and inferior forms of life.

In its effort to understand this unfeeling and sometimes hostile world, science has frequently attempted to subdue and dominate it. Psychologically, this aggressive approach has served to reinforce, in mainstream scientific methodology, the stereotyped male traits of toughness and competition. And this, Roszak suggests, has resulted in a clear-cut gender bias. At its most obvious, this gender bias, until very recently, led to the almost total exclusion of women from the scientific professions—even after our society at large had long since emerged from the prefeminist era. At a more subtle level, gender bias created what Roszak calls "macho science," a scientific methodology from which qualities regarded as "feminine"— sensitivity, gentleness, warmth, compassion, and intuition— were excluded.

Roszak believes gender bias may have influenced the ways in which we understand the very atomic foundations of nature. I will leave it to the physicists to judge if he is right about that, but speaking for my own field of study, this macho science has been largely responsible for the way scientists treat animals.

This is evident in the science training of students, who become victims of a kind of brainwashing that starts all too often when they are small children and is intensified, in all but a few pioneering colleges and universities, throughout higher science education courses. By and large, students are taught that it is ethically acceptable to perpetrate, in the name of science, what, from the point of view of the animals, would certainly qualify as torture. Students are encouraged to suppress their natural empathy and are persuaded that an animal's pain and feelings, if they exist at all, are utterly different from our own. By the time these students are qualified as professional scientists, they have been programmed to accept animal suffering and to justify their actions on the grounds that the research is for the good of humanity. The very fact that scientists seldom question the ethics of using other animals for our own good is a superb example of human arrogance—reinforced, I must add, by the species-ist views of many Western religions, which also have been traditionally male-dominated.

Recently women have come into their own in many fields of scientific endeavor, particularly in the study of animals in the wild. Louis Leakey, my mentor, who had faith in me when I was young and untrained, believed women made better observers. While this is by no means always the case, I believe that women demonstrate a number of traits, possibly innate, that may give them an advantage over men in certain forms of research. First, a woman raising her family in the traditional way needed patience; mothers who were more patient were likely to be more successful parents. Second, mothers had a real need to understand the needs and desires of nonverbal animals, namely their own babies before they could speak. And third, women have traditionally played a major role in maintaining peaceful relationships among members of their families. This was only possible if they were acute and intuitive observers, quick to notice and understand sudden changes of mood and subtle communication signals.

When I began my chimpanzee study in 1960, there was no prescribed scientific methodology for collecting data in the field. I had not been to university at the time, but Leakey, wise beyond his time, believed that to be an advantage. I would not be biased by the reductionist thinking of mainstream science. I not only studied the chimpanzees, but allowed them to teach me. I tried always to record behavior objectively, but I discovered that the power of intuition could be a scientific tool for understanding, provided the insights this revealed were rigorously tested afterward. Above all, I was free to describe the personalities, moods, and emotions of the amazing beings with whom I had the privilege of working.

The chimpanzees taught me that, although we humans are indeed a unique species, we are not as different from the rest of the animal kingdom as we once thought. We are not, after all, the only beings capable of rational thought, of emotions like happiness, sadness, despair, and of mental as well as physical suffering. This is humbling and helps us better to understand our own place in the nature of things. The greatest scientists, through the ages, have believed that science is more than simply asking questions, gathering and interpreting facts, or proving theories. The exploration of the world around us should also enrich the soul, make us more fully aware of our humanity, and humble us with feelings of awe as we gaze into the night sky, swim in the coral reef, or allow ourselves to be utterly at one with the green, entwined, and mysterious world of the rainforest.

For the past decade I have been putting much energy into developing a program called "Roots and Shoots," which addresses itself directly to the issue of scientific sensibility. Roots and Shoots involves young people from kindergarten to university in hands-on activities that demonstrate care for their environment, whether wilderness or city, for nonhuman animals, domestic and well as wild, and for the human community—all this with the goal of making the world around them a better place. The movement strives to teach young people the interconnectedness and interdependence of all life forms— "deep community," as Theodore Roszak calls it. Roots and Shoots represents my attempt to share with young people around the globe something of the knowledge I acquired from my years in the forests. And too, something of the magic that I knew as a child when, supported by my remarkable and understanding mother, I learned to respect all living things and the environment we all share. Above all, the philosophy of Roots and Shoots stresses that every individual, human and nonhuman, matters, and that each one of us makes a difference. It is my hope that children who develop a deep respect for animals and the environment and who are empowered to take action may, as they become adults, help to guide tomorrow's world away from selfishness and greed and in the direction of understanding, compassion, and love. In such a world, science would be free of gender bias, and adolescent boys would no longer feel, as they so often do today, that concern for animals and the environment is "just for girls."

Such a world, Theodore Roszak believes, holds out hope for a new scientific sensibility based on the traditionally "feminine" respect for all life: "sympathetic relatedness," as he describes it. He believes that the future of our species and the fate of the

Earth depend upon such a deep psychological and moral transformation. He is right. Without fundamental changes of this sort, life on our planet as we know it is doomed. It is imperative that we pause to listen to the distress of the Earth, adapt our societies to meet its needs, cure its hurts with the sympathy and compassion that, throughout history, have been perceived as feminine virtues. Science must acknowledge the role of these virtues as we move through the next century.

The Gendered Atom, by bringing this issue forward, makes an important contribution to the thinking of our time. Its message should be heeded by every scientist, and indeed by everyone who is concerned about the grim state of our planet as we enter a new millennium.

I

frankenstein, feminism, and the fate of the earth

I heard a shrill and dreadful scream. It came from the room where Elizabeth had retired. The scream was repeated, and I rushed into the room. Great God! why did I not then expire! She was there, lifeless and inanimate, thrown across the bed, her head hanging down, and her pale and distorted features half covered by her hair, her bloodless arms and relaxed form flung by the murderer on her bridal bier. The murderous mark of the fiend's grasp was on her neck, and the breath had ceased to issue from her lips. . . . While I still hung over her in the agony of despair, I happened to look up. With a sensation of horror not to be described, I saw at the open window a figure the most hideous and abhorred. A grin was on the face of the monster; he seemed to jeer as with his fiendish finger he pointed towards the corpse of my wife.

WE ARE AT THE CLIMAX of Mary Shelley's *Frankenstein*. The gloating monster hovers above his helpless female victim, ready to ravish, to kill. She is at his mercy. She screams, she struggles . . . in vain. The hero arrives too late. His lady love lies expiring upon the bed.

I suspect all of us can recall scores of images like this from movies we have known since our childhood. The zombie, the werewolf, the mad slasher carrying off the half-clad leading lady . . . can we imagine a horror story that does not include a frightened female swooning in the monster's arms? We can see the moment coming miles ahead. Yet how disappointed we would be if it did not come. Somehow the dramatic truth seems to demand it.

The damsel in distress was already a cliché of the Gothic novel when Mary Shelley sat down to write *Frankenstein*. The "shilling shockers" on which the children of her day grew up—the pulp fiction of that era—invariably featured voluptuous ladies in filmy nightgowns chained to the dungeon wall or cowering in the shadowy crypt, fearfully awaiting the ghost, the ghoul, the walking corpse who would soon have his way with her. But *Frankenstein* added something new. In this case, the hero is a scientist, a new social identity never before explored in fiction. He stands at the center of the tale, the man of reason swept away by a twisted passion that is at once intellectual and sexual. The female-victim is his bride, murdered before the marriage can be consummated. The monster is a creature of the hero's own making, in effect his unnatural son. Bonds of filial and matrimonial love tie the characters together, connecting them all to "a workshop of filthy creation," as Mary Shelley called the first experimental laboratory to appear in literature.

By a stroke of genius, she transmuted the creaky Gothic tale into the first true science fiction. Borrowing from a genre once populated with monsters of the past—demons, imps, and witches—she discovered a new species of horror that belonged uniquely to the future of scientific society.

Yet as original as Mary Shelley was, her story is permeated by an archetypal familiarity—as if there were a mythic resonance about the lurid scene we see unfolding in this bedroom, something as primordial as the concept of taboo. *Frankenstein* may anticipate the latest developments in genetic engineering, but the tale is haunted by a temptation that reaches back to the Book of Genesis: "*. . . and ye shall be as gods.*" That was the prophetical warning Mary Shelley placed at the heart of her tale. Science, though it champions reason, can degenerate into mad rationality. For all its idealism, it does not dependably elevate us above sin; in the wrong hands, it may only enhance our power to do evil.

Sigmund Freud believed we harbor childhood memories of parental intercourse in the depths of the unconscious. He called this the "primal scene." He was convinced that this image, which children usually interpret as a violation of the mother by the father ("an attempt to overpower the woman"), was not a true personal recollection but a "phylogenetic possession," something remembered from the prehistory of our species.

Can there be other primal scenes that are just as powerful? I believe there is at least one, an image that returns to us every time we watch the monster menacing the maiden. In this case, the violation of female by male takes on a larger dimension. What we are witnessing in that encounter, even when it appears in the most vulgar context, is the rape of nature.

This is a journey through the strange sexual subtext of modern science. It connects elements of physics and biology with insights from the new field of feminist psychology. Taking its cue from Freud, it regards no metaphor as a "mere" metaphor, but as a window into the soul. With the same insistent curiosity that psychiatrists have brought to bear on art, religion, and social custom, it asks why all of us, scientists included, continue to speak of nature as *She* and God as *He* as if we did not "know" better. At its most searching level, it seeks to understand why "mother" and "matter" were once thought so closely interwoven that the same word was used for both. Before we finish, we will learn how the atom, the hard core of the hardest science, was transformed into a gendered object and how several generations of male scientists, by willfully blinding themselves to that fact, came to believe they had at last arrived at a true vision of the world, only to see that vision at last become shadowed by monsters.

This is admittedly a highly speculative undertaking. Any project that delves into the depths of the human unconscious has to work from hunches, hints, and the free play of the imagination. Psychology has always had more literary art to it than its practitioners care to realize. Think how often the keenest insights into human psychology have been found in literature. Don Quixote's delusionary pursuits, Othello's murderous jealousy, Captain Ahab's obsessive vengefulness. . . . In these pages, *Frankenstein* performs the same role in feminist psychology that the Oedipus story plays in the theories of Freud: mythology coming to the aid of psychological inquiry. If one grants the necessity of risky conjecture, I believe the findings presented here are strong enough to be made part of our understanding of what science is—and what it is not.

For many readers, especially scientists, it may seem improper to subject science to an analysis of this kind. Scientists have done such a thorough job of portraying themselves as the guardians of rationality that many of them may believe they—uniquely—have no psychology at all. Is this not what we have been taught to honor as the scientific method—a way of seeing the world that is wholly unblemished by subjective taint? Ideally, the scientific mind should be a purely rational instrument, solidly logical to the core. Only theology purports to be as capable of speaking with divine authority, free of personal feeling and historical context. In real life, nothing remotely like that kind of detachment is humanly possible. Nor, I suspect, would many scientists enjoy being the sort of person they must pretend to be when they write for a professional journal or deliver a paper before their colleagues. On such special ceremonial occasions scientists, much like priests performing Mass, seek to make themselves wholly transparent before the divine eye.

The poet William Wordsworth brilliantly captured that reverential image of science in a passage from his lyric autobiography *The Prelude*. At Cambridge, where he went to school in the 1780s, there was a statue of Sir Isaac Newton, the founding father of modern physics. It stood in the university chapel. Looking back to his youthful years, this is how Wordsworth remembered that famous work of art:

> And from my pillow, looking forth by light
> Of moon or favoring stars, I could behold
> The antechapel where the statue stood
> Of Newton with his prism and silent face,
> The marble index of a mind forever
> Voyaging through strange seas of Thought, alone.

In these few lines, Wordsworth captures the somber and principled isolation of scientific man as only poetry can. As a young girl, Mary Shelley might have heard the poet himself read this passage. Wordsworth was often a guest at her family's many literary soirées. Daughter of the radical philosopher William Godwin and the feminist firebrand Mary Wollstonecraft, she grew up in one of the most literate and intellectually daring families in England. She might have gone to bed one night pondering that "silent face," that "mind forever voyaging." She might have fallen asleep hearing that final, sorrowing epithet "alone . . . alone . . . alone" echoing away into the darkening void. She may have wondered if we should want the human mind to be such a "marble index," chilly as stone, eternally perfect . . . but never alive.

Science has changed vastly over the centuries. Newton's physics, hailed in Mary Shelley's day as a true reflection of the mind of God, has been all but turned inside out. Where Newton saw simplicity and solidity, his intellectual heirs now see a quantum phantasmagoria filled with paradox and uncertainty. We have come to regard his mighty principles and finely wrought formulas as merely a special case within the far larger, more complex universe we inhabit. Nevertheless, the underlying spirit of Newton's quest remains unchanged. Science still aspires to an objectivity that outlaws the irrational.

One can try one's best to force the irrational out of mind, but that is repression, not objectivity. And to confuse repression with objectivity leads us to that ominous identity called the "mad scientist," the man so out of touch with his own imperfect motivations that he becomes emotionally and morally anesthetized. Perhaps that is why some of us cannot be assured too often that, beneath their professional exterior, scientists really do have private lives, that they can be as conflicted and confused as the rest of us. When James Watson, the codiscoverer of the DNA double helix, digresses to let us know he has an eye for pretty girls ("popsies," as he calls them in his memoir), it may add nothing to his biology, but it encourages us to believe there is a human being behind the biology who might be expected to have a conscience.

These days we are fortunate to have a new style of science writing that seeks to put a human face on its subject. Thanks to biographers who go out of their way to emphasize quirky biographical details, we are discovering that scientists also have their emotional eccentricities. Sometimes what we learn is little more than gossip: that Stephen Hawking keeps a picture of Marilyn Monroe over his desk, that Richard Feynman loved to play the bongos, that Albert Einstein had a love life outside his marriage. Other revelations can be unflattering but nonetheless forgivably human, as for example when we are told how egotistically ambitious scientists can be, how petty, how nasty, how driven by the same lust for fame and fortune we associate with other celebrities.

Finally there are the revelations that tell of severely troubled lives: the hypochondria that turned Darwin into a recluse, the depression that drove Ludwig Boltzmann to suicide, the sexual guilt that led Allen Turing to the same sad end. Turing, one of the founders of computer science, once proposed a "test" that would measure how close artificial intelligence had come to the real thing. He wondered what one might ask in a structured conversation to decide if one's interlocutor was a human being or a computer. The question is still debated, but the ultimate Turing test might be to pose the question "How would a guilt-stricken homosexual commit suicide?" Would a computer ever conceive of eating an apple laced with cyanide? Probably not, but Turing, the consummate logician, chose just that bizarre way to end his life.

As candid as scientists have become about their emotional side, few among them would grant that their personal idiosyncrasies have significantly distorted their impersonal search for truth. For example, no one would suggest that there was a direct connection between Boltzmann's suicidally depressive condition and his theory of entropy, even though entropy, taken to mean that the entire universe is running down, does wear an air of tragedy. Conclusions like that would clearly be reaching too far. Suppose, then, we grant that the standard scientific method—being fiercely logical, making conscientious measurements, honoring the empirical evidence, remaining open to criticism and counterarguments—effectively screens out emotional distortion. Nevertheless, modern psychology has taught us that the unconscious contains more than purely personal contents. There is a collective unconscious made up of cultural elements that are absorbed into the personality in the cradle, if not before. These contents include imagery and mythic materials, values and suppositions so basic that they can seem self-evident and are rarely reflected upon with any critical awareness. Consider the following:

- there is a real world "out there" beyond one's own mind
- touching things proves they are really "there"
- other people exist as separate centers of consciousness
- time moves forward in a straight line with causes coming before effects

- reality is best studied by the rigorous application of logic to empirical facts (or, quoting Galileo, "the book of nature is written in the language of mathematics")

- the past, which we can never know directly, was governed by the same forces we can study around us now

- human beings have the right to experiment on "lower animals"

- the less emotionally involved we are with what we study, the more accurately we understand it

None of these are "facts" or "findings." They are assumptions that may lead to facts and findings. And, like all assumptions, they are open to doubt. There are traditions highly honored in other societies that have called one or another of them into question. The Buddhists, for example, can be rigorously logical in their analysis of experience, but the conclusion they reach—that the self is illusory, that the void is more "real" than the sensory world—would provide a very different starting point for doing science. One can live one's entire life unaware of the way in which culturally transmitted elements like these shape the contours of the mind.

Take the most basic metaphor in modern science—namely, that there are "laws" of nature. I daresay few scientists have ever sorted through all the philosophical baggage that this concept carries. Behind this commonplace notion lies an immense cultural tradition from which we learned that the universe was created by a lawgiver God who, as father, lord, and master, dictated the orderliness of nature, which is a lesser material realm under His jurisdiction. Science bootstrapped itself into existence on

the basis of that familiar Sunday school lesson. In the early days
of the scientific revolution, the idea of natural law helped two
generations of natural philosophers work out their first quantita-
tive ideas of motion and gravitation and chemical interaction.
In the beginning, to understand nature was to read the mind of
God, on the assumption common to all good Deists of the time
that God's strict adherence to logic guaranteed the regularity of
the cosmos. Later, agnostic scientists, themselves under the
influence of other philosophical ideas, edited the great lawgiver
out of the picture; but they retained the laws.

There seems to be an unwritten agreement in professional
science to leave troubling philosophical matters like this
undiscussed, the better to get on with one's research. The scientist who loiters over "the reality of Reality" or the strict
meaning of determinism or randomness may never get down
to work. That way lies philosophy, for which there are no
prizes handed out at Stockholm. But sweeping such matters
out of sight does not automatically build a mental firewall that
screens them from consciousness. On the contrary, it is a principle of modern psychology that the feelings most apt to influence behavior are those that we try hardest to suppress. They
work like malicious secret agents in the shadowed corners of
the psyche. The basic strategy of every school of psychology is
therefore to recover the repressed, to shine the light of awareness upon all that is hidden so that its influence can be
assessed and allowed for. This amounts to saying that honesty—a clear declaration of one's tastes, preferences, vested
interests, and emotional involvement—may be more important than objectivity, if by objectivity one means affecting a
blank and neutral state. In that latter sense objectivity may be a
pretense that hides profound distortions.

The first person to raise the possibility that science has an unconscious dimension was not a psychologist but a poet. William Blake developed a critique of the Newtonian science of his day that was based on the assumption that the mind is a profoundly conflicted faculty—a place of "mental fight." Blake deeply admired science; he never failed to portray it heroically. But he was concerned that science saw the universe from an odd angle that hid as much as it revealed. Science screened the value of things, the beauty of things, the sacredness of things as if these qualities might not really be there. Blake called this Single Vision, and contrasted it with his ideal of Fourfold Vision: an understanding that included the poetic, the sensuous, and the visionary along with the rational. Because he favored a fuller, more complex conception of knowledge, he fervently prayed for our culture to be saved from the scientist's severe abbreviation of reality: "God us keep from Single Vision and Newton's Sleep."

A century later, Freud was frank to admit that Romantic artists like Blake had discovered the unconscious well before he had. But because Freud regarded himself as a man of science, he could hardly adopt Blake's unsettling view of the scientific psyche. Science provided Freud with his method and his guiding imagery. He represented the psyche as if it were a steam engine, driven by energies and pressures that needed to be "converted," or "discharged," or "channelled." Far be it from Freud to discredit the claims of professional objectivity.

Ironically enough, the figure who was prepared to do that began his career as a behaviorist, a leading figure in the school of psychology that has always purported to be even more scientific than Freud's psychoanalysis. Abraham Maslow, eventually to become the founder of humanistic psychology, spent the greater part of his life in the psychology labs of Brandeis University. In the latter part of a distinguished career, Maslow found himself troubled by the fact that so many of his experiments involved deceiving his subjects and seeking to manipulate their conduct. At a certain point he began to question his own motivations, always a risky move for a professional scientist.

Maslow's honest doubts led to the first effort by an academically trained psychologist to understand the role of the unconscious in science. His *Psychology of Science: A Reconnaissance* (1966) was an impressively original work that raised disquieting issues. For example, Maslow suggested that science was unconsciously dominated by a method of inquiry that was grounded in fear and therefore governed by the need to control. Control usually took the form of predictability. Pressed too far, that need could become a "cognitive pathology" that distorted more than it illuminated.

As he probed deeper into the matter, Maslow began to see connections between the psychology of objectivity and the character traits of stereotypic masculinity. Like other men, male scientists could also be burdened by "the inflexible, neurotic need to be tough, powerful, fearless, strong, severe." Their fear of seeming "soft or mushy" at a certain point could then "turn out to be a defense against (misconceived or misinterpreted) femininity." In his own field of psychology, Maslow felt the key move in that defensive strategy was to "atomize" the person under study. As he put it, "the search for a fundamental datum in psychology is itself a reflection of a whole worldview, a scientific philosophy which assumes an atomistic world—a world in which complex things are built up out of simple elements."

While Maslow was convinced that "atomistic dissection" was out of place in the human sciences, he never questioned its validity in physics or chemistry. It did not occur to him that atomism might be as cognitively pathological in the hard sciences as in psychology. We had to wait until a distinctly and deliberately feminist psychology appeared in the 1970s before doubts of that kind could be raised. Only then did we begin to see how pervasively gendered modern science is.

It takes little effort these days to recognize the distortions wrought by gender bias in our society. Even scientists blush to realize that no more than a few generations ago, when talents as bright as Marie Curie were being denied an education, their male chauvinist predecessors regarded women as frail, small-brained, hysterical, squeamish little things unsuited to the laboratory or the classroom. Since then, matters have improved. Even so, a recent study by Margaret Eisenhart and Elizabeth Finkel concludes that women who go into the sciences are still expected to "act like men." But at least such studies get published and the issue can be laid before the public. What continues to go unnoticed, however, is the possibility that the sexual politics underlying that fact may influence our most basic understanding of the physical universe. Physics itself and the entire quantum worldview that provides its dominant paradigm may have been seriously warped by motivations that remain so effectively repressed that scientists have no awareness of their presence.

I have met scientists who are admirably candid about their own preconceptions and prejudices. They admit that scientists have been caught lying and cheating or filching one another's results. As our culture's official guardians of reason, they deplore the fact that science has its internal politics, its fads, fashions, and fixations. But I have met few who have been willing to consider the possibility that assumptions about sex and gender have shaped the most basic tenets of their work.

Perhaps, then, it takes a historian to observe the obvious. Namely, that the theories, methods, and sensibilities of Western science have, for four centuries, been under the control of an exclusively male guild. For the greater part of that period, the society that shaped every scientist great and minor was male-dominated through and through. That society took all that was male to be "normal," whether in politics, art, the economy, scholarship, social ethics, or philosophy. As Londa Schiebinger has argued, "At the core of modern science lies a self-reinforcing system whereby the findings of science (crafted by institutions from which women were excluded) have been used to justify their continued absence." How could that fact not make a difference to the theory and practice of science? Why should we assume that the study of nature is the one pursuit that has escaped being gendered?

Scientists like to think of their field as "self-correcting." That is a comforting belief. It amounts to saying scientists can never be wrong—except temporarily. But in truth there is no such thing as a self-correcting field of knowledge. *People* make mistakes; and *people* correct those mistakes. Often an entire generation of diehards has to go to the grave before the new, corrected version of truth can emerge. That has happened as often in the world of science as in art, theology, or scholarship. Eliminating bias from the things we believe requires unstinting self-criticism. The only way we can hope to know anything beyond ourselves with certainty is to know ourselves first. In our time, scientists are seeking to formulate a Theory of Everything that will produce ultimate knowledge. That is probably a futile pursuit; "everything," after all, covers a lot of ground—shoes and ships and sealing wax, cabbages and kings. But if there is any sense to such a project, it will be possible only when we can *see* everything.

Feminist psychology contends that science cannot know the whole of nature because scientists are themselves not whole, no more so than the rest of us. For that matter, the Romantic artists from whom Mary Shelley took her inspiration in writing *Frankenstein* bore more than their share of psychic wounds. Artists have as much of a reputation for madness as scientists do. The man Mary Shelley shared her life with was a lifelong neurotic who wandered in and out of mania and dark depression; he often woke up screaming in the grip of some hair-raising, drug-induced hallucination. Indeed, in looking for a living model for Victor Frankenstein, Mary fixed upon Percy, as if to ask what might result if a man of science were ever swept away by the Faustian passion for limitless experience she could see in her lover.

Mary Shelley deserves to be remembered among the founders of feminist psychology, though in no professional sense. She was a storyteller and mythmaker whose role was to give psychology some of its most fruitful insights. She had no idea she was foretelling the fate of the Earth when she wrote *Frankenstein.* Her prophesy emerged unbidden as part of a Gothic thriller, using the framework of a newly popular genre. But in her day, a woman was up against certain limits. Her publisher thought it would be unbecoming to place a woman's name—and so young a woman at that—on so shocking a tale. Submissively yielding to anonymity, she settled for insinuating herself into the book. She tells the story through three male voices—Victor Frankenstein; his nameless monster; and Robert Walton, the sea captain to whom Victor relates his tragic history. But she cleverly masked her own pervasive feminine presence by arranging the entire narrative in the form of letters that have been collected by Walton's sister. The sister is known to us by the initials MWS. These are, of course, Mary Wollstonecraft Shelley's own initials. Her mind is the enveloping matrix within which the tale unfolds.

What would *Frankenstein* be like if Mary Shelley had been able to draw upon her full feminist sympathies? In writing *The Memoirs of Elizabeth Frankenstein*, that was the question I set out to answer, at least as well as a male author might. But that meant sharing as much as I could of Mary Shelley's life and times, especially what she had experienced during the uncanny summer of 1816 when she first looked into the face of the monster who continues to haunt us all. So I set out to follow in her footsteps. Yet even before I had completed my research, I found my thoughts straying well beyond fiction. I realized I needed more than a novel to delineate how science, in its impassioned search for power, has twisted our relationship to nature. Where had would-be scientific benefactors like Victor Frankenstein lost their moral bearings? How had their well-scrubbed and brightly lit laboratories come to replace the haunted crypt and Gothic dungeon as places of terror? Above all, how might science regain its ethical balance and once again become, in Francis Bacon's words, "a gospel of hope"? Fiction can dramatize, but it cannot gracefully analyze, questions like these.

I had set out to track the Frankenstein myth back to its place of origin on the shores of Lake Geneva. I finished with these reflections on the soul of modern science. If they make some contribution to restoring our love and loyalty for the Earth that mothered us into existence, I can think of no better way to give Mary Shelley the voice she could not assume in her own time.

Controversy raises hackles, especially when it strikes at professional pride. There will be those in the sciences who will not like what they read here. One response to confronting things with which one strongly disagrees is to begin setting up straw men to knock down. So let me anticipate.

Do I believe scientists are any more vulnerable to bias than anybody else? Not at all. There is nothing here that could not be said of every other academic discipline including my own field of history. But bias in science is far more serious because science functions as the supposedly objective worldview of our society. If science tells us that the natural world is an alien, meaningless collection of inferior and unfeeling objects with which we have no ethical relationship, that has perilous consequences. In a time of environmental crisis, it is apt to lead to treating the world with an irresponsibility we cannot afford.

Am I saying that science is so fundamentally flawed that it has produced nothing of value? Hardly. I take science to be the most distinctive and intellectually valuable enterprise of Western society. The atomistic vision of nature, the main focus of this essay, was a daring if brutal transfiguration of the everyday reality people had known for millennia. By reducing the world to nothing more than bits of matter in random motion, atomism helped teach us how to talk about nature mathematically. That is a formidable achievement and an enduring contribution. But given the unconscious motivations behind atomism, the exclusivity of that approach has cost us dearly. Feminist psychology invites us to see the world in a different, more personal and warmly relational way. If this book persuades people to consider accepting that invitation, it will have been as successful as I could expect.

Do I think that every scientist has been guilty of gender bias? Not at all. I know too little about individual scientists to make such a judgment. My interest is in the collective identity of science, meaning that which can be assessed by its methods, guiding paradigms, protocols, and underlying presuppositions. It is science *as an institution* that I focus on here. As we have learned with respect to class, race, and ethnicity, institutions can be dominated by hidden agendas that are invisible to those who work within them. Institutions can take on a life of their own. In that sense they can become Frankensteinian monsters that run out of control. When institutions take over from people, people relinquish their responsibility. And that is when the worst damage is done.

Am I saying that all scientists have subscribed to atomistic reductionism and its underlying sexual politics? Of course not. Science is hardly a monolithic enterprise; it has its camps and schools and internal debate. There are scientists who have, for one reason or another, been uncomfortable with the atomistic vision of the world. Since the days of Galileo, scientists have argued constantly about the foundations of the natural world. Is the world a continuum or an aggregation? Is matter viscous or granular? Is the universe a pail filled with molasses or a bag filled with marbles? There have always been a marginal few who questioned the validity of the atom. There were even scientists who fiercely rejected the atom because it was too "materialistic." But in that debate, atomism has been more than merely another talking point; it has been the dominant paradigm of physical reality. It *felt* right to the vast majority of scientists long before it could be proven right—which in fact it never was. Even so, it has been made to fit even where it was ill-suited. Most importantly, it has served as the model of bedrock knowledge that scientists should adopt in all other fields of study. And that is where I suspect deeper, repressive forces are still being brought into play. Even after the classical atom had lost its intellectual currency, the masculine bias it expressed was there to carry on.

Finally, and perhaps most important of all, do I believe the insights we gain from Mary Shelley's *Frankenstein* and from feminist psychology mean that science must now adopt a new feminine bias that swings in the opposite direction? Given the strong feminist orientation of my argument, some might be quick to believe I am calling for something as simplistic as that. They might even conclude that I favor a return to the feminized nature symbolism and magical rites of Paleolithic times. There are some in the women's movement who sincerely believe something like that is possible. In my eyes, nothing could be more futile. It makes no moral sense to me to overcome one bias by substituting another. Our goal must be a bias-free, nongendered science.

As a historian, I tend to want to salvage value from the past. In that spirit, I join with many ecologically oriented feminists in believing that the prescientific imagery of the old Earth Mother religions expressed a remarkable intuitive appreciation of natural systems in nature. On the basis of that perception, our ancestors created an ethic of reciprocity that environmentalists like Aldo Leopold have reconstituted as a sound scientific "land ethic" for our time. Similarly, I believe the traditional symbol of the *Anima Mundi*, the feminine soul of the world, did a better job of prefiguring the complexity we are now discovering in nature than the atomistic paradigm that dominated the early modern period of Western history. But there is no direct way in which our culture can appropriate that long lost worldview. Though we can take our bearings from the past, we need our own paradigm—and a richer one than either machines or mother gods can offer us.

All of which is only to say that truth does not arrive full-grown; we limp toward it across a field of errors. All of us see the world through a glass darkly. We advance toward the light by wiping that glass a little clearer for those who come after us. The changes that are coming over science in our generation—the growing appreciation for complexity and self-organization, the deepening recognition of structure and pattern at both the cosmic and quantum level—are significant departures not only from primitive atomism, but from the physics and astronomy that dominated the early twentieth century. Science grows, science changes. But these new directions still face resistance from an inherited compulsion to reduce nature to its parts and dominate it as a whole. My hope is that I may be able to illuminate the origins of that compulsion and diminish its pernicious influence.

T. S. Eliot believed that "humankind cannot bear very much reality." But he might just as well have added "humankind cannot bear very much self-deception either." If we were not able to free ourselves of repression, if we did not wish desperately to do so, neither psychology nor the religious act of confession could ever have come into existence in the first place—and there would be no point in writing a book like this. If anything, the commitment to demonstrable truth on which scientists have set their hearts may help them to see reality more readily than those whose beliefs have no respect for evidence of any kind. But by the same token, the great pitfall for scientists is to believe they have a method that uniquely and automatically guarantees they will transcend prejudice and preconception. That is not methodology but ideology, and in the grip of ideology even great scientists may blind themselves to truths that simple honesty and a modicum of humility would make obvious.

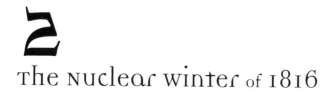

2

The nuclear winter of 1816

> The bright sun was extinguish'd, and the stars
> Did wander darkling in the eternal space,
> Rayless, and pathless, and the icy Earth
> Swung blind and blackening in the moonless air
> > Lord Byron, "Darkness" (1816)

On the night my wife and I arrived in Geneva, there were storms over the Alps. The thunder rolled along the lake in long, bellowing waves that were violent enough to shake the walls around us. Gazing from the window of our hotel after the power failed, we could see the sky and the mountains lit for miles each time the lightning flashed. It might have been midday, except that the light was a ghastly gray that drained everything of its color. The next day at breakfast people at the hotel told us this was the worst storm they had ever seen.

This was how Geneva had welcomed Mary and Percy Shelley on the day they arrived in 1816. As Mary remembered the journey in her diary, they crossed the Jura Mountains "by the light of a stormy moon" and were soon enveloped by gale and blizzard. "Never was a scene more awfully desolate," she wrote. It had been a foul summer. Across western Europe, ponds froze in August and crops failed. There were food riots everywhere as the famine spread. Though Mary could not have known it, the storms she encountered were part of a worldwide phenomenon, a darkening of the sun that had changed the global climate. In history books, 1816 is called "the year without a summer," almost as if the birth of the world's archetypal mad scientist had to be accompanied by an ominous turn in the weather.

Now in the summer of 1994 Betty and I had come to Geneva so that I might put the finishing touches on a novel. After studying and teaching *Frankenstein* for some thirty years, I had finally decided to join countless other novelists and filmmakers in adding my own variation to the classic theme. Keeping such close emotional company with Mary for so many years, I had come to think of the novel I was completing as the climax of a literary love affair. In my mind she would always be the daring young woman who so fully embodied the vibrant Romantic spirit of her age. She was frozen for me in that identity. Now, as that affair was drawing to its end, I felt I must visit the place that had inspired her, if only to share some greater measure of what she might have experienced in giving birth to the modern world's most enduring myth. Was it a good or a bad omen that Geneva was greeting me as it had greeted her, with all the atmospherics of a Hollywood thriller?

❄ ☉ ❄

W HEN SHE BEGAN writing *Frankenstein* in 1816, Mary was not yet Mary Shelley. She was still the unwed, though no longer virginal, Mary Godwin — or at least that was the name her father assigned her. Later in life, after she married and took the name "Shelley," she dropped "Godwin" and added the maternal "Wollstonecraft." She switched names as a deliberate effort to associate herself with her mother, the founder of modern feminism, a "hyena in petticoats," as her conservative critics called her. Still in her teens as she approached Geneva, Mary had already spent three years living (and traveling) in sin with the embattled Percy. As Percy's mistress, she had undergone a miscarriage at age sixteen and then given birth to a second illegitimate child at eighteen. That summer, Percy, hounded by creditors and an estranged wife, decided to flee into self-imposed exile. He took Mary and their newborn son with him. The nearly penniless young family made their way by foot and by mule across fields where battle scars of the Napoleonic wars were still fresh. An era of political upheaval was reaching its violent end all around them. They were heading for Switzerland, where they had heard Lord Byron would be summering.

These days, we think of Switzerland as the home of cheese and chocolate, luxury hotels and secret bank accounts, a tiny toy music box of a country distinguished by its placidity. But in Mary's time, Switzerland had a very different image. It was Europe's first wilderness, the remote beginning of our modern environmental awareness. People did not come to Switzerland to shop for cuckoo clocks in those days, even though it was the watch-making capital of Europe. They came for the mountains.

For the first time in Western history, mountains had become objects of aesthetic contemplation, and the more rugged the better. Artists came to paint them, exaggerating their forbidding desolation. The paintings circulated among the elite classes like travel brochures. Along with the highlands of Scotland, Switzerland became a sight to see for its rough-hewn grandeur and remoteness.

Percy had come seeking ecstasy in the Alps, and he found it. Before he left, he would write *Mont Blanc*, one of the greatest nature lyrics in the English language. Byron too would be moved to produce one of his finest works. With Percy, he had rented a boat to sail Lake Leman. His *Prisoner of Chillon*, a celebration of "the eternal spirit of the chainless mind," was inspired by a sailing trip the two poets made to the hoary castle that guards the eastern edge of the lake. If nothing more than these two classic Romantic poems had come of that Swiss sojourn, we might remember the occasion.

But Mary, who had never published a word, was destined to write a stranger and greater work than either of the poets. How she came to create the most memorable of all Gothic novels is a treasured anecdote in English literature.

As luck would have it, Percy, Mary, Byron and their party had little chance to enjoy the Alpine vistas they had come to see. For the most part, unseasonable cold and fierce rain squalls forced them to keep to the villa that Byron had rented on the outskirts of Geneva. To amuse themselves, they read Gothic tales to one another by the fireside. And when they had read all the stories they could find in the library, they agreed to create their own. Though Percy was troubled by ghastly nightmares, he never succeeded in capturing them on paper. Byron toyed with a ghoulish tale that some believe was the first vampire story, the distant source of Count Dracula, but he left the fragment unfinished. Only Mary, like the good schoolgirl she was, finished the assignment. The ghastly yarn she would take home to England to complete was occasioned by a late-night conversation between Byron and Percy. The two poets were discussing the possibility of reanimating dead bodies. Percy, ever the scientific enthusiast, was convinced the feat could be done by the use of a mysterious new force called animal electricity. The Italian scientist Luigi Galvani had shown that an electrical spark might make the legs of a dead frog quiver. Percy and Mary had attended Galvanic exhibitions where they had seen the limbs of dead animals twitch and the faces of hanged criminals grimace when their bodies were touched with an electric charge. Perhaps science was that close to the secret of life.

As Mary remembered it, her novel arose from these amateurish scientific speculations. But the bad weather that penned the English visitors indoors and gave rise to their macabre conversations provides an even more uncanny connection between modern science and the creation of *Frankenstein*. We have Carl Sagan to thank for making the association.

In the 1970s, at the height of the arms race, Sagan brought a terrible prospect to the public's attention. He called it "nuclear winter." He was convinced that in the wake of a thermonuclear war, the dust clouds that would be blasted into the atmosphere might blot out the sun, cool the planet, and blight most of the food chain on which life depends. Sagan was warning us that our weapons of war had reached the point of deranging the planet's natural forces. Was there any evidence that a catastrophe so vast might really happen? There was, but it was an act of God, not man.

In April 1815, a volcanic island in the East Indies named Tamboro erupted. Geologists believe it was the largest explosion to take place on the planet in at least ten thousand years, several times more powerful than the better known eruption of Krakatoa in 1885. The dust that was scattered twenty miles skyward by Tamboro disrupted weather patterns around the globe. Before the year was out, sunsets in England had turned stunning red and purple—inspiring the landscape painter Joseph Turner to change his palette. The following summer Europe was gripped by unseasonable rain and cold.

This was the weather that confined Mary and her friends to their villa. In a very real sense, her inspiration might be said to have burst from the bowels of the Earth. The story of the first mad scientist was imagined by a young woman kept indoors by storms that are now used to model the devastation that might be wrought by thermonuclear war. Dr. Frankenstein was born of a freak of nature that presages Dr. Strangelove.

3
The Largest scientific machine in the world

There were two locations I knew I had to explore in and around Geneva. Both played key roles in the creation of *Frankenstein*. One was Belrive, the lakeside district Mary chose for the Frankenstein country estate. In her day, Belrive was a fishing village made up of small farms and peasant hovels. It might then have taken hours to make the journey to Geneva over rutted roads. Today Belrive is a quiet, upscale suburb with none of the bucolic charm Mary must have found there. There is, however, one remarkable building she would have known, a chateau built for the Seigneur of Belrive in the seventeenth century. Today this handsome palace is owned by the Aga Khan and guarded by a formidably high wall. *"Défense d'entrer"* reads the sign on the high iron gate. But on the day Betty and I came calling, the gate was unlocked, so we invited ourselves in and furtively began walking the grounds. Fascinated with the atmosphere of the place, I made rapid sketches and rather recklessly peered in at windows to take notes. I have no idea how I would have explained myself had we been caught trespassing. I suppose I would have tried something like "I'm an author doing research." Fortunately nobody spotted us. I found the chateau itself a suitably Gothic setting for the youth of Victor Frankenstein and immediately appropriated it for my novel—though I decided to relocate it in my imagination some eight miles to the east and south, well up into the rugged Voirons Mountains.

The second site I needed to see was more important. It was the house where Mary dreamed *Frankenstein* into literary existence. The Villa Diodati still stands on the hills above the lake, about twenty minutes by car to the east of the city. Privately owned now as it was when Lord Byron rented it, the estate is closed to the public. But on our visit to the neighborhood, Betty and I were in luck. Once again, the gates had been left open, and so we stole in to investigate the still gracious mansion. Eventually we made our way through the deserted gardens to the terrace that stands outside the bedroom windows. In her journals, Mary later described that summer as the time when she had "walked out of childhood into life." I tried to imagine her as she might have stood at one of these windows in the early morning, surveying the magnificent mountains that span the northern horizon.

But Betty noticed a more remarkable sight. "Do you know what we're looking at?" she asked as she pointed across the lake.

She had recognized that the Villa enjoys a direct sight-line upon CERN on the French-Swiss border. CERN, the *Conseil Européen pour la Recherche Nucléaire,* houses the giant particle accelerator that has given scientists their most intimate view into primal matter. At CERN even atoms rank as huge. The machinery that has been put to work there has smashed the physical stuff of the universe into far smaller, more ephemeral bits, at certain points achieving for mere trillionths of a second exotic states of energy that never existed on the planet. At CERN scientists have gazed back across the eons to recapture the birth of matter as it occurred in the Big Bang.

Built in the shape of a circular tunnel 100 meters under-ground and twenty-seven kilometers in circumference, CERN's mammoth LEP (Large Electron Positron) accelera-tor runs under several small towns in France and Switzerland, including Ferney-Voltaire, where our hotel was located. That was why Betty and I had scheduled a visit to the laboratory while we were in Geneva; it is one of the great sci-entific wonders of our time. From the terrace outside the Villa Diodati one looks directly across Lake Geneva to a spot that would mark the center of the buried accelerator. Thus, if Mary, waking from bad dreams of mad doctors and monsters in the summer of 1816, went to her bedroom window to gaze out at the distant mountains, she would have been looking at the future site of CERN. Her dream, as she recalled it, was of "a pale student of unhallowed arts" and of "the thing he had created." And how, at last, was this unnatural being brought to life? "Upon the working of some powerful engine. . . ."

The first thing she would see the next morning was the destined home of "the world's largest scientific machine."

Was this second sight? As steeped as I was at the time in Gothic fantasy, I could not help but wonder. I might eventually have dismissed the uncanny geographical alignment of the accelerator and the villa as a mere coincidence and remembered our visit to CERN as no more than a side trip. But something about the power and the mystery of the LEP collider haunted me. I was certain there was some significant affinity between Mary's monster and the great machine. I think now I know what it is. Whether or not Mary was blessed with prevision, her story adumbrates the project most associated with CERN: the curious scientific fascination with smashing atoms, and what that project has done to our understanding of the universe.

AT CERN THE violent disintegration of matter has been taken to the "quark level," 10^{-18} meters, a millionth of a billionth of a centimeter. There is no way to make a mental picture of so minuscule a dimension; one simply accepts it as a mathematical calculation. Trying to imagine such subatomic minutiae violates the first rule of modern physics: "never visualize." These are not such objects as the eye was evolved to see. "Particles," the very word used for the evanescent entities that scientists find at these inconceivable depths, is misleading. Most nonscientists understand a particle to be a "thing," small but tangible, like a mote of dust or grit. But the particles that scientists study are not "things" at all. They are more often spoken of as "waves" or "wave packets," "events," or even "ill-defined smears." In superstring theory, one of the more esoteric schools of physical thought, particles are said to be vibrations on tiny strings that fold in ten dimensions. To my amateurish way of thinking, such a fanciful reference to sound played upon strings provides a better grasp of subatomic reality than vision. I have come to think of particles as musical notes that are palpably "there" the way a chord struck on a piano is "there": a measurable physical pulsation in the air that becomes a momentarily sharp and well-defined tap upon the ear, then rapidly spreads and dissipates. That is as subtle as I can imagine the material world becoming, and still it is not as subtle as physics would have it. One can find ruminations about angels in medieval theology that seem more grossly physical than the "probability clouds" that materialistic scientists are examining in our time.

Reaching that delicate level of investigation is achieved by machines that are not the least bit delicate; the engines that have laid bare the physical rudiments of nature are always described in terms of their violence. One of the first atom-smashing accelerators was ominously named SPEAR, for Stanford Positron Electron Asymmetrical Ring. SPEAR's stated purpose was to "kill" electrons. The massive LEP accelerator at CERN is vastly more proficient at killing particles. Able to "strip," "hurl," and "blow to pieces" the particles that pass through it, the LEP produces collisions of particle beams traveling at close to the speed of light. In films that show the scientists at work on the accelerator, we see serious men (and they are almost all men) sometimes wearing hard hats and heavy boots as they clamber up towering machines, connect bulky cables, hack away at computers, then finally sit waiting for near-ghostly particles to have productive accidents.

This is industrial-strength science surrounded on all sides by metaphors of force. In a recent essay, one atomic physicist described his work with an accelerator in words that reveal the glee that comes of controlling such power. He begins: "Blam! Blam! Blam! Blam! The shots echoed down the hall at the Lawrence Livermore National Laboratory. . . ." Is there any limit to how far science can travel along the road of violent disintegration? As powerful as it is, the LEP accelerator is already scheduled to be superseded by CERN's Large Hadron Accelerator in about 2005. That may be as large a machine as CERN can build, but it still falls far short of what some high-energy physicists call their "supreme [though possibly unreachable] goal": an accelerator capable of mustering a hundred billion, billion, billion electron volts. In principle, such a machine would be able to overcome the energy that combines the four basic interactions of matter. The result would be the ultimate act of disintegration, particles ripped out of all relationship to one another and at last, so we are to assume, revealing their most closely guarded secrets.

I know it will sound frivolous, but these ever-so-serious matters remind me of nothing so much as a favorite game I played as a child. The boys would gather to slam little toy cars and trains into one another at the highest speed our arms could achieve. The objective was to catch a glimpse of some spectacular leap or turn. "Let's play collision," someone would call out. And the game went on for hours. But all we were left with at the end was a heap of broken parts. A nuclear accelerator is far more fruitful. It scatters the parts so that each can be "seen" by a detector emerging separate from the rest.

One of the most dramatic of these quests at CERN occupied several years of theory, preparation, and machine-building during the 1980s. It was the search for the W and Zed-zero particles, entities so rare that billions of invisible collisions were required to jar loose just a few of them from the binding core of the atomic nucleus. For weeks, scores of scientists monitored the machine around the clock. The theorists had predicted the particles were there, and after the experimentalists had hurled opposing beams of particles against one another again and again, they found what they were looking for: just the right streaks of light on a few photographic plates. The event was announced to the world amid high celebration. Champagne was uncorked and a press conference called. It was the discovery of a world within a world.

The methods and the machines used for research like this are new, but the program being pursued at CERN dates back to the beginning of modern science. It is called reductionism. The name comes from "reduce," in this case to reduce the complex to the simple, the big to the little, the whole to its parts, if necessary by smashing the whole until nothing but its parts remain. Reductionism holds that the best way to understand the world is to break it down into its smallest units and then see how they are put together. There is a seeming practicality to reductionism that can be intimidating to its critics. Reductionists get *into* things; they insist on finding out what's *really there*. Things have parts. Get hold of those parts. Find out how they work. See how they fit together. Is that not how engineers look at things? Take it apart, put it together. Discover what makes it tick.

As a philosophy, reductionism can be traced back to ancient times. It appeared in fourth-century b.c. Athens as a school of thought that held an original notion: Everything in the cosmos is made of tiny bits that cannot get any smaller. These were called *atoms*, "that which cannot be divided." An ingenious concept but nothing more than a concept. The Greeks had no way of studying anything smaller than a crumb. Nevertheless, assuming the existence of nothing more than these invisible little objects, the atomistic philosophers asserted that one could explain everything: why fire burns and water flows, why wind and thunder and rain behave as they do, how the eye sees and the ear hears, why things live and die. Modern scientists think of Greek atomism as refreshingly "scientific." The atomists were, after all, talking about purely physical objects, atoms that were invariant in size and weight, subject to exact laws of motion, and having no quality that could not be reduced to quantity.

On the surface, this looks like a precociously lucky guess about the nature of things. That guess has given the atomists an honored place in the history of science. One prominent interpretation holds that the Greeks might have invented science two thousand years earlier in Western history. But then came the Dark Ages. Men lost their nerve and reason faded. Promising truths like atomism were thrown into eclipse by ignorance and intolerance. Religion, the enemy of reason, crucified the intellect and set back the progress of human thought by centuries. Two prominent television series — Jacob Bronowski's *Ascent of Man* and Carl Sagan's *Cosmos* — have endorsed that picture of the past. They overlook the fact that, like all Greek philosophers, the atomists were human-centered thinkers. Man was the measure of all things for them, including the study of the cosmos.

Tough-minded scientific atheists like to think only philosophical softies turn to religion for cosmic consolation. They might do well to read more history. The atomism they prize so highly was not pursued as pure research but as the search for *ataraxia*, peace of mind. It was religion, not science. It has remained religion in the sense that it is still a satisfying belief based upon "the evidence of things unseen."

In actuality, the earliest atomists, Democritus, Epicurus, and Lucretius, seized upon atoms because they wanted to make their followers happy — or at least tranquil. They taught that believing in fickle, temperamental gods led to anxiety, fear, and guilt. On the other hand, believing in impersonal, law-abiding atoms made one feel secure: Nobody up on Olympus was out to get you. "The reason why all mortals are so gripped by fear," reasoned Lucretius, "is that they see all sorts of things happening on the Earth and in the sky with no discernible cause, and these they attribute to the will of the gods." The solution to human misery was a totally logical, totally impersonal world system: atoms moving in the void according to fixed laws. Atomism dispelled even the fear of death, because death was nothing more than the dissolution of the whole into its original, undying parts. "A thing never returns to nothing," Epictetus announced, "but all things after disruption go back into the first bodies of matter."

The atom entered history as a tiny, philosophical tranquilizer, an intellectual solution to our deepest emotional dread. For the atomists, technical questions about the objective characteristics of matter counted for far less than finding ways to relieve anxiety. For example, take a typical question that was much debated by the ancient atomists: Are atoms strictly determined or do they have some degree of freedom? One might mistake that for a purely scientific query. But the answer was actually dictated by what felicity seemed to require. Democritus thought people would find strict determinism more consoling, so he said the atoms were bound by law. But his disciple Epicurus believed such rigid determinism was depressing. Seeking a jollier tone to life, he allowed for spontaneity: Atoms, he said, could (unaccountably) swerve — just a little, but enough to allow some trace of free will. That was the spirit of ancient atomism. It was therapeutic, not scientific.

Atomism has been part of our culture for so long and has been so forcefully endorsed by modern science that it is easy to overlook what a bizarre idea it is. After all, no Greek atomist ever saw an atom. By their very nature atoms were invisible. The ancient philosophers had no idea how atoms might stick together. Was it by means of tiny hooks, perhaps? Fifteen centuries later, when atomism was revived in the days of Galileo and Newton, atoms remained as speculatively nonempirical as ever. They were never "found"; they were conjectured into existence. They were as completely hypothetical as the six biblical days of creation. Newton had no trouble assimilating them into scripture. "God in the beginning," he proclaimed, "formed matter in solid, massy, hard, impenetrable, movable particles." The authors of Genesis would have raised no objection. They could easily have accommodated Newton's "corpuscular philosophy." *And God said, "Let there be atoms."*

In the early nineteenth century, the English chemist John Dalton seized upon atoms as a way of making chemistry mathematical. Atoms could, in principle, be weighed and counted. That made them a good basis for calculating chemical formulas. Dalton's work on atomic combining laws (how atoms stick together) and the creation of Gregor Mendeleyev's periodic table seemed to bring the Newtonian world order to its grand culmination. The periodic table, which now hangs in the front of every high school chemistry lab, suggested that the only difference between the elements was a matter of weight. Quality could be reduced to quantity.

It was all marvelously simple. Atoms gave the visible world a purely physical foundation. They supposedly moved in response to the same mechanical laws that neatly predicted the movements of the heavenly bodies. There was a difference, of course. Heavenly bodies could be seen; atoms could not. But atoms offered something more valuable than visibility. Finality. They were the bedrock of reality. Religiously inclined scientists might wish to believe that God had created the atoms and set them in motion, but atheists were just as free to assert that atoms were eternal and required no God to make or move them. In either case, there was nothing more to explain in nature beyond them or below them. That was what made them "basic."

The Catholic catechism I memorized in my childhood began with the question "Who made the world?" The answer was "God." The next question was "Who made God?" The answer was "nobody made God. God always was." Atheists have long chastised theologians for failing to explain where God came from. Why stop there? they ask. But atoms reside at exactly the same cutoff point in atheist ideology: "Nobody made atoms; atoms always were." If one asked what the world was made of, the answer was: isolated, autonomous, imperishable, colorless, odorless, tasteless, self-contained objects that fall into a strict periodic pattern and obey the universal laws of motion. This is what the word "physical" meant through the first three centuries of modern science. This is why physics came to be considered the "hardest" of the hard sciences: it works closest to the fundamental stuff of the universe. Atoms were what proved that materialism was right—dead right.

That was exactly the issue the Romantics took with the Newtonian philosophers of their day. They believed that an arrogant, aggressive materialism was driving all enchantment from the universe. Atoms were colorless, soulless, unlovely things. They lacked magic. That was why William Blake protested in behalf of the spirit. After all, what were these wretched atoms compared to the glories of true religion?

> The atoms of Democritus
> And Newton's particles of light
> Are sands upon the Red Sea shore
> Where Israel's tents do shine so bright.

Romantic poets may not have been scientists, but they had a good empirical point. How could such drab, shapeless entities remotely explain the lively, sensuous world we see around us? After all, if it is in the nature of isolated atoms to collide and rebound, how did any of them ever cling together to form all the well-shaped, functioning things that are the most obvious features of the world: elephants, fig trees, diamonds and rubies, you and me? Nineteenth-century scientific speculation on the matter easily became ludicrous. Some theorists still thought Lucretius might be right about the tiny hooks that held atoms together; others believed atoms might come equipped with something like suction cups. Or perhaps they were selectively magnetic. Still others suggested that gravity fastened one atom to the next, but without explaining why the gravity that supposedly held rocks and metals together did not make water and gas just as solid.

Conjecture like this was little better than overweening nonsense, and Romantic poets were not the only voices to cry out in protest. Eventually, philosophers of science as eminent as Ernst Mach and Henri Poincaré made it abundantly clear that there was no way to achieve a smooth reduction of big, complex objects to tiny, bouncing atoms. The observations, the measurements, just did not fit. Lord Kelvin, among the most respected physicists of his day, struggled with the concept of the atom throughout his scientific life, finally dismissing it as some-thing based on "incredible assumptions." He claimed that "chemists and other reasonable naturalists of modern times, losing all patience with it, have dismissed it to the realms of metaphysics."

Well before the end of the nineteenth century, Kelvin began searching for a different kind of atom. It was a desperate quest. Like Michael Faraday before him, he soon found himself brainstorming wholly disembodied atomic models. Faraday was the first to think of the atom not as a material point without internal structure, but as some kind of "field." This was a puz-zling new use of a word that had previously been used for a piece of land or a battleground. A field was not a location; a field was a place one located things *in*. But now, as with the word "wave," originally a rippling ridge of water, science was about to borrow from the common vocabulary and radically transform what it borrowed. For Faraday, a field was a sort of ethereal plain extending to infinity across which invisible cur-rents ("tubes of force," as he called them) might exert influ-ence. For the first time, Western science was speaking of matter not as a thing in a place, but as an area of activity that had to be grasped as a whole.

Kelvin eventually came up with another idea about the atom. He preferred the image of a complex, vibrating vortex, an idea he developed after watching smoke rings in the air. Neither his hypothesis nor Faraday's gained approval, but ideas like these pointed prophetically in an unsettling new direction, toward "matter" that was neither solid, nor tangible, nor uniquely locat-able: matter that was, in fact, nothing like the matter materialists had been talking about for two centuries. Kelvin went to his grave believing the prevailing mechanical model of the atom—

a solid, resilient little billiard ball—to be a total failure. But most scientists continued to pretend atoms were really there and that they provided the basic explanation for everything. Like all true believers, materialists can be stubborn.

But all the while, nature was becoming elusive in exactly the way that scientists hate. It was losing its hard edge and becoming unmeasurably messy. The atom was behaving as if it had an *inside*; and odd things were going on in there. Spectral lines and vibrational degrees of freedom were being detected, phenomena that suggested inner workings: not a solid state, but *things related to things*. Among those who had gone farthest in studying these disturbing new phenomena was the French physicist Pierre Curie. Eventually, in league with his talented wife, he would uncover transformations taking place inside the atom that hinted at an alchemical level of malleability. The Curies had a strange but revealing married life, one that hints at issues of gender as complex as the issues of physical theory raised by their research. All the while the couple toiled to understand the mysteries of radioactivity, Pierre insisted that Marie keep the babies and their family affairs strictly out of his way. He subscribed to an almost priestly conception of science. The disorderly domestic side of life was Marie's to cope with. As he saw it, his work as a scientist was a "life opposed to nature," a hard discipline in which "we give all our thoughts to some work which removes us from those immediately about us." In that pursuit, he believed, "it is with women that we have to struggle, and the struggle is nearly always an unequal one. For in the name of life and nature they seek to lead us back." Yet Marie, who was left to feed and diaper the babies, finally contributed as much as Pierre to the rise of a new physics.

Finding the hidden order of things has always been the goal of science. But how do we know "order" when we see it? That has to do with how our faculties have been schooled. Aldous Huxley once observed that the Western vision of nature arises from a "well-gardened" European vantage point. No one who was born in the tropics, he felt, would turn out to be a Newton or a Wordsworth. In a steamy, dangerous world filled with fevers, crocodiles, and swamps, nature is too chaotic and too sinister for poets to admire or scientists to understand. Huxley, who did so much to popularize ecology in the 1950s, actually sympathized with this dread of tropic disorder. How could anybody find beauty in the jungle? "It is fear of the labyrinthine flux and complexity of phenomena that has driven men to philosophy, to science, to theology—fear of the complex reality driving them to invent a simpler, more manageable, and, therefore, consoling fiction." In this context, for "fiction," read "atom."

Huxley's use of "men" in this passage is surely gender specific, based on an image of the tidy laboratory as male turf. Experience shapes perception. The laboratory and classroom train perception in one way, the jungle in another . . . and the home in still another. Those who have traditionally been assigned to watch over the daily turbulence of the kitchen and the kitchen garden, the toilet, the nursery, the barnyard, and the bedroom—they are called "women"—live in an environment that leads them to expect little in the way of neatness, order, or clarity out of life. Perhaps they cannot help but cultivate an astute awareness of loose ends, subtle nuances, and ragged relationships. They may even learn to accept disorder as an integral part of the real world, which is the world we settle for. At least one scientist believes that our recent willingness to study the strange new contours of Chaos Theory had to wait until the gender bias of modern science had weakened sufficiently to allow a shift in perception. "Chaotic behavior," Stephen H. Kellert observes, "was screened off from study by a procrustean form of attention that was paid only to elements of the world that could be reduced to objects for human use." That utilitarian bias, he believes, was the result of a masculine preference for the orderly and predictable.

These days, if you confront scientists with the neat, primitive atomism that dominated Western society through the nineteenth century, they are likely to wince with embarrassment. They might even try to pretend that nobody ever really believed in such a thing. But that would not be true. For three centuries the foundations of scientific theory in the Western world stood upon a body of thought that not only had no empirical verification, but was theoretically inane. That is an important fact to remember whenever we are told that science is "self-correcting." It may be; but it would seem that self-correction is compatible with being wrong for a very long time before the correction sets in. Classical atomism is an example and hardly a trivial one of exactly that: being wrong for a very long time.

4

The psychology of the quark

Though I dearly wished to do so, I was not given the chance to view the LEP collider at CERN. That is the holy of holies, restricted to those who, like the high priests of ancient temples, approach with the appropriate credentials. It is a reasonable restriction, but it does lend an air of the esoteric to the uniquely "public knowledge" that science purports to offer. I had to settle for next best: hearsay. One day aboard a touring boat that had taken us to visit Chillon, Betty and I met an English theologian who knew a scientist at CERN. He had been invited to inspect the sanctuary. Exploring the cool and echoing tunnels had been a memorable experience for him. When he described the great chamber where the accelerator resides, his voice fell into a reverent hush. He described what he had seen as an "underground cathedral."

Odd that he should have put it that way. My own fanciful image of this modern temple of the nuclear mysteries is

very much like that. I have come to think of it like the prehistoric caves at Lascaux. In ancient times, those who studied the wonders of nature also took to the underworld,
seeking contemplative quiet and darkness. We have no
counterpart for the natural philosophers of the Paleolithic
period, a combination of artist, visionary, and shaman. The
subjects of their curiosity were the great beasts they lived
among and hunted. With infinite care, they drew bison,
deer, wild horses, and mammoths on the stony surfaces,
working by smoking oil lanterns or rushlights. Some scholars think they created their images by blowing liquified
charcoal across the stone, as if to breathe the breath of life
into their subjects. The haunting paintings that cover those
walls are nature as the earliest members of our species knew
it ten thousand years ago.

The machines at CERN, hidden in their own well-
guarded cavern, also produce a kind of art: squiggles and
smudges that resemble modern action painting. The pictures are the tracks left not by scampering animals, but by
the "particle zoo," the more than 300 creatures of pure
energy that leave their photographic trails in a chamber of
chemical clouds. We do not think of the deep particle realm
as living; it is the world of the physicists, not the biologists.
But had Percy Shelley known of the quanta, I think he
would have had little difficulty reading vitality into them. In
his early atheist days at Oxford, he was already pondering the
implications of a nontheistic universe. In his vivid, lyrical
imagination, the physical world was no less sentient than the
ensouled cosmos of the alchemists. Science led Percy toward
a kind of atheistic pantheism that recognized the higher destiny of the most rudimentary matter.

Today, science has a word for what Percy had in mind: emergence. Emergence is nature's capacity to evolve wholly unpredictable new forms of ever-increasing complexity. We now believe the stars, galaxies, and galactic clusters emerged in all their intricate splendor from mere dust, and so too living tissue from lifeless chemicals. These forms must have been inherent in the initial conditions of matter, but how they unfolded remains an enigma.

Principled materialist though he might have been, Percy drew upon science to deepen his worship of all being. In his first published poem, he had already embraced the "affections and antipathies" of atoms and particles.

> There's not one atom of yon earth
> But once was living man. . . .
> I tell thee that those viewless beings,
> Whose mansion is the smallest particle
> Of the impassive atmosphere,
> Think, feel, and live like man;
> That their affections and antipathies,
> Like his, produce the laws
> Ruling their mortal state;
> And the minutest throb,
> That through their frame diffuses
> The slightest, faintest motion,
> Is fixed and indispensable
> As the majestic laws
> That rule yon rolling orbs.
>
> *(from* Queen Mab, *1813)*

If the new shamans at CERN ever feel the need to carve an inscription above their accelerator, they might consider

Percy's hymn to the emergent vitality of matter. After all, would not a true Theory of Everything have to explain how hydrogen, the humblest of elements, has managed, in its own good time, to turn into people?

AS LATE AS THE 1880s, scientists were still describing the atom, especially in the popular literature of the day, as a small, hard sphere of matter analogous to a very tiny grain of sand. Textbooks offered imaginary drawings of these invisible entities, showing them as little circles, often shading them or filling them with dots to differentiate one element from another. Where the atoms combined to produce a chemical compound, the molecules appeared as collections of balls packed together like a group of marbles in the middle of the floor. What held them together? Why did these identical things take on such different characteristics when they were grouped together? Nobody could say. As we have seen, a few scientists of the day found this conception of the world so bizarre that they insisted it was purely hypothetical. Nothing like these tiny billiard balls could possibly account for the durable variety of real things we see around us every day.

Nevertheless, atomists stuck stubbornly to their guns, insisting that absolutely everything could be explained by the gyrations of these little balls, including a whole range of phenomena that was coming under ever more discriminating investigation: light, heat, magnetism, spectral lines, electricity, and radiation. In these areas, atomists had to confront serious reservations among their colleagues. Some physicists were coming to feel that nature might be radically divided between "corporeals," for which atoms offered a reasonable explanation, and a growing inventory of "incorporeals," which could not possibly be explained by the random movement of uniform billiard balls. So fascinated did scientists of the period become with incorporeals that they were invoked to explain the supernatural. Sir William Crookes was convinced that spiritualism, a great craze of the day, could be traced to one or another of these incorporeal substances. Spiritualists claimed that ghosts were made of a subtle fluid called "ectoplasm." Crookes was certain that the fluid was a form of cathode radiation.

Still other scientists argued that energy was more basic and more empirical than any purely material object. The debate between atomists and energeticists is a significant difference of opinion, but oddly enough the energeticists were not all that distant in spirit from the atomists. Energy, as some then understood it, was still a point-location. But instead of a point encased within a hard physical shell, they preferred a point vibrantly surrounded by an invincibly repulsive force field. That was what made the atom impenetrably hard: energy actively pushed other things away, at least over a small distance. The entity in this case might be a fuzzy ball of energy, but it remains an isolated location, a thing apart and without relations.

Then, in the 1890s, a new possibility emerged. Perhaps the atomists had been right all along, except in one respect. They had not pushed their theory far enough. Perhaps there was a far tinier atom than anyone had suspected. The English physicist J. J. Thomson had isolated a strange sort of particle that was thousands of times smaller than hydrogen, the simplest of all the classical atoms. He called it an "electron," because it carried an electrical charge. Were these mysterious little objects the true foundation-stones of the material universe? Was everything made of electrons? The trouble was, electrons did not behave like physical things. Under certain circumstances, they acted like nothing but a ghostly electrical charge whose location could not be fixed. Matter, it seemed, was being dematerialized by the sciences. The more closely physicists looked, the more rapidly the atom evaporated into a haze of probabilities. Yet our everyday experience was that this immaterial stuff held together tenaciously and made the world solid and durable.

Given the enormous, centuries-long investment that scientists had in the billiard-ball vision of the universe, it is to their credit that they honored the physical evidence before their eyes. Even when they could make no sense of what they observed, they recorded what they found and left open all questions of consistency. There can be no clearer way to distinguish science from other fields of inquiry than this stubborn commitment to observable data. That took courage, because the worldview that had launched science along its historical course was quite simply collapsing. As one historian puts it, "physicists had lost their grip on reality." The atom was not solid, it was not final. But that did not put an end to their hope that some truly atomistic particle might yet be found.

The experiments of Ernest Rutherford just before World War I were decisive in this great shift. He clearly proved that the atom had an internal configuration. The imagery that guided his work is particularly interesting. He was the first to use the military analogy of "shooting" a particle at an atom to blast out its internal parts. He liked to describe his experiments as an "attack" on the atom. The result was a revelation. The atom was not a lump made up of smaller lumps that were the true, underlying atoms. Rather, it was an intricate structure of things and forces that resembled the solar system with its planets circling around the sun in a vast void. The things Rutherford found inside the atoms were not simply some smaller variety of the old, free-falling atom. They were subtly organized. And it was this organization that in some way accounted for the durability of matter. Though the search for a true final particle continued, some physicists were beginning to suspect that the relationships between things—the pattern, the structure, the design— counted for more than any one piece of matter.

Since the latter part of the nineteenth century, science has shown the Newtonian atom to be a figment of the theoretical imagination. It never existed; there were never good grounds for believing it existed. The nucleus of the atom has proven to be more and more porous, as each newly discovered part reveals a deeper internal structure. "Atoms, like galaxies," the historian of science Timothy Ferris tells us, "are cathedrals of cavernous space." And like cathedrals, they have an exquisitely complex architecture that grows more baroque as we search deeper into the atomic nucleus. Or perhaps it would be a better choice of metaphor to say that the atom has opened out to reveal an infinitesimal world system as subtly complex as any ecosystem in macroscopic nature. One might almost think of the atom as having an ecology, a coherent pattern of connected parts.

This is what Nobel laureate Steven Weinberg means when he says, "out of the fusion of relativity with quantum mechanics there has evolved a new view of the world, one in which matter has lost its central view." The matter he speaks of is the atom of Newtonian physics. As that matter melts away into fields and patterns, we are beginning to learn that *everything in nature is organization, structure, relationship.* Nothing stands as an island; the most fictitious identity in all creation is that of the solitary individual or the isolated atom.

Which brings us back to CERN. Currently, at the level where the CERN accelerator works, physicists are finding particles so tightly organized that only undreamt-of force can separate them and then at times for no longer than a few fleeting instants briefer than quadrillionths of a second. These are the quarks. But unlike the atoms of old, quarks come in a variety of kinds and they come together in "families," a curiously convivial phrase. Quarks give up their family connections stubbornly, and then decay in a micro-instant, as if they had no way to survive out of relationship. But still the atom-smashing continues. Laboratories around the world now seek to outdo CERN in power so they can blast their way ever deeper into the nature of the quark. The Brookhaven Relativistic Heavy-Ion Collider can produce as much as twenty trillion electron volts of energy. Battered by such great engines, the quarks are themselves becoming a menagerie of exotic creatures possessing "color," "flavor," "charm." The names are fanciful, as if to signal us that these are not really "things" anymore. They are, as the physicist David Bohm has expressed it, "concentrations and knots in a fundamental, continuous field." That is not a very clear concept; it is surely nothing the mind can visualize. This is simply to say something is "there" in space that makes matter solid, even though that "something" is not itself a solid object.

No one has ever witnessed free quarks. One science writer tells us that they have been "locked up inside nuclear dungeons" since ten micrcoseconds after the Big Bang. "Quark confinement," the force that holds quarks together as a unit, must be a built-in feature of physical reality. Quarks are not things, but a system, a radically real system. Even if some way were found to blast them apart, their natural state may always have been an integrated whole. The long search for the ultimate, simple, solid "thing" has yielded what CERN scientists call "patterns that interlock to infinity."

Is there an ultimate particle, an end point with no internal structure? Some physicists believe that leptons (the family to which the electrons belong) and quarks are ultimate, but others speculate that even they are composed of still tinier constituents called preons, leptoquarks, or squarks, all nested one within the other like Russian dolls.

Suppose, then, we were to blast the quark apart. Would that give us the true uncuttable atom? In 1997, a new particle, an exotic meson, was discovered at Brookhaven. The result of five years of "slamming atoms together," as one report put it, the new meson was found in the debris that resulted from one of the most powerful collisions ever achieved at this level of physical reality. The particle, which is supposed to reveal how quarks stick together, lasted for a trillionth of a trillionth of a second. A *trillionth of a trillionth of a second.* Does time, on that scale, have any reality at all? Is it possible, the layman's mind wonders, that beyond a certain point, what we are learning is that matter does not *want* to be taken apart?

Of course that is to anthropomorphize. But there are physicists who have begun to doubt that much more can be learned by building bigger colliders to stage bigger collisions. They ask if the results of further physical disintegration may represent diminishing returns: one learns *less.* If a particle can be segregated for only so brief an instant, maybe it is part of a larger whole that needs to be accepted as "basic." The effort to find something more "fundamental" destroys the more basic phenomenon, which is relatedness. Instead, a more delicate approach to disassembling matter may be the way forward in exploring the intricacy of the quantum world. That is the goal of CEBAF, the Continuous Electron Beam Accelerator Facility at Newport News, Virginia. CEBAF's function is to deal gently with matter; Timothy Paul Smith describes it as "tickling" and "nudging" the protons it studies with a finely tuned exploratory beam. In comparison to "blasting" and "smashing," words like "tickling" and "nudging" sound almost affectionate.

Whatever comes of these new, more refined research techniques, they are certain to lead us further away from the classical simplicity of Newton's physics and deeper into the complexity of nature. And that raises a great question. *Why did we ever take the atom seriously as a scientific concept?* Why did people as undoubtedly brilliant as most scientists are spend so long a period of time clinging to an idea for which there was no verification and which was theoretically nonsensical? How can we account for the extraordinary appeal of the classical atom?

Freud once asked a question very much like that about religion. He asked, if religion is as obviously wrong as rational people can see that it is, why then has it survived so long in human culture? Freud's conclusion was that religion offers certain benefits that have nothing to do with reason. Religion, he concluded, is "a defense against childish helplessness." Believing in "the benevolent rule of a divine providence" protects us "from the necessity of defending oneself against the crushingly superior force of nature." Psychiatric illusions, Freud pointed out, are not simply mistakes; they have an emotionally supportive function.

It may seem odd to introduce a psychological formulation into a discussion of high-energy physics, the most objective of all branches of science. But that is where my exploration of *Frankenstein* at last brought me. In taking up an investigation of the scientific psyche, I am following where one of the deepest critiques of science has led me.

It is called feminist psychology.

How seriously one takes the application of feminist psychology to science depends upon how greatly one believes scientists are influenced by the contents of the unconscious mind. Some might wonder if scientists, as the most rational of human beings, really have an unconscious mind. And even if they do, does not the scientific method guarantee that it will never impinge upon their professional work?

In recent years, feminist psychologists and feminist historians of science have dared to answer that question with a resounding "No." The scientist's psyche is as vulnerable to irrational promptings as any other, and perhaps more so, since scientists take such staunch pride in their invincible rationality. Exploring the scientific unconscious as boldly as Freud ever probed our erotic impulses, feminist psychologists have discovered a deep sexual warp even in the hard sciences, a bias that arises from the peculiarly masculine character of professional science. The connections are complex and elusive, but they suggest that our understanding of the universe is gendered down to the level of the *prima materia*.

Feminist psychologists have been struck by the remarkable correspondence they see between the characteristics of the classical atom (which, we must remember, was never observed because it never existed) and the stereotypic characteristics of the male personality. Descriptions of the male *persona* as it presents itself in psychological theory are filled with terms like "autonomous," "separate," "isolated," "self-determining," "rigid," "insensitive." Feminist psychologists call this character type the "separative self," contrasting it with the "self-in-rela-tion" that girls are raised to respect. Like the classical atom, the separative self is solid all the way through, admitting of no internal division, no unconscious or irrational dynamics. It is, in the words of the feminist theologian and psychologist Catherine Keller, "armored against the outer world and the inner depths." For such a self, "intimacy, emotion, and the influence of the Other arouse its worst anxieties." It is often this very sense of isolation and self-reliant autonomy that finally brings men into therapy. In the great crises of life, fol-lowing a death or a divorce, they seek some way to form caring, sensitive relationships, especially with women. Tired of bounc-ing about in a chilly void, they are looking for warm, human companionship.

Recall that the founders of modern science were all men, and often heavily patriarchal men. Henry Oldenberg, the first secretary of the Royal Society, the seventeenth-century proto-type of all later professional associations in science, made it the highest priority of the new organization to establish a "Masculine Philosophy." The concomitant to that project, as he saw it, was to root out "the Woman in us," an astonishingly frank and revealing phrase. Seeking an ever more fundamental understanding of nature, might not men, biased so strongly against the feminine, intuitively subscribe to a paradigm that reflected their own personality? Add to this the domineering sexual metaphors that have haunted science from its begin-ning, constant references to nature as female, and to science as an effort to control and conquer her. Are feminist psychologists so far from the truth in seeing a powerful masculine bias not only in science as a profession, but in science as a worldview?

Could this be the source of the classical atom: a projection of the nonrelational, separative self upon nature? Does that same psychological twist underlie our continued effort to reduce natural phenomena to *something* hard, final, and isolated?

This is what Evelyn Fox Keller has in mind when she concludes that science is based upon "a historically pervasive association between masculine and objective, more specifically between masculine and scientific." She sees traces of compulsive masculinity in some of the most crucial and abstruse debates in the history of scientific thought. As an example, she cites the concept of the "field," as it was formulated by Faraday. This rich theoretical idea now has a central place in modern science. But it was at first stoutly resisted. It seemed at odds with the basic material structure of the world. Fields were all about ethereal patterns and lines of force. Some scientists could muster the daring to adopt them, but most could not. In this Keller sees a reflection of the discomfort many male scientists experience with ideas that leave "the boundaries between subject and object . . . never quite rigid." As one commentator on Keller's insight puts it, "Keller links the disinclination of scientists to admit to such an ambiguous reality to the process of gender differentiation, arguing that the male child, in our gendered culture, comes to see the mother as essentially different from himself. This gender differentiation then lays the foundation for the scientist's later objectification of the archetypal female, Mother Nature."

In Keller's view, "the network of gender associations in the characteristic language of science" is "neither natural nor self-evident. . . . These are not just ornamental images on the surface of scientific rhetoric; they are deeply embedded in the structure of scientific ideology, with recognizable implications for practice."

"Practice" can cover a great deal of scientific territory. It might include the sort of medical science that continues to analyze the human organism into smaller and smaller atomistic parts, rather than seeking to balance the whole. It might take the form of the multibillion-dollar human genome project, which is based on the assumption that genes, like the classical atom, are isolated elements of reality at discrete locations that can be mapped and manipulated. Perhaps "practice" even includes the fascination among physicists with the aggressive use of big machines like accelerators and colliders to find the ultimate atomic particle. In all these cases there is a strikingly similar fixation upon disintegrating patterns into constituent parts that are supposedly more "real" and can be reassembled and reshaped to the desire of the inquiring mind.

That assumption, once it becomes second nature to people, can have far-reaching consequences in every walk of life. There is one area of experience where it may have exerted a powerfully formative influence upon every member of Western society. Through the seventeenth and eighteenth centuries, as midwives were being either ridiculed or persecuted by the male medical establishment, child rearing was undergoing a quietly revolutionary change. Male physicians were becoming the official baby doctors of our society. When Mary Shelley was born, it was a male doctor who took over Mary Wollstonecraft's troubled delivery and proceeded to infect her with the fevers that killed her. In the view of the new obstetrics of the early modern period, pregnancy was a disease; women had to be treated as enfeebled patients, often constricted and given chloroform so that they could not "interfere" in the birth. Midwives had used a birthing stool on which the mother sat during the baby's delivery; the posture seemed to welcome the child into the world using the full force of the Earth's gravity. With the midwife in charge, delivery was a communal experience, carried out with many women relatives present to greet the newborn. Male doctors preferred to isolate the mother, strap her down, sedate her, and use forceps, an instrument that it was considered unbecoming for a woman to use.

Once the baby was born, the practice in the best modern hospitals was to remove the child at once from the mother and place it in the care of professionals. The mother might be so heavily drugged that she was in no condition to handle the baby. For the past two centuries, medical science has required newborns to be whisked off to an environment as different from the womb as possible. The child is wrapped tight and left on its own, lying on a firm, sterile surface in a brightly lit, noisy maternity ward, surrounded by other distressed babies. If they cry, let them. It will teach them to accept their lonely condition all the sooner. What is the effect of all this but to break the bond between mother and child as early as possible, as if to force the child toward autonomy?

At its extreme, this procedure produced the Skinner Box of the 1950s, an invention of the highly respected behavioral psychologist B. F. Skinner. Skinner advocated placing the newborn in a dry, sterile, well-lit, wholly controlled, almost clinical environment immediately after birth and for most of the first year of life, all in order to protect it from the mother's germs, irrationality, and general incompetence. Here proper conditioning could begin. He saw this as the scientific mode of child-rearing. But in the judgment of child psychologist Jean Liedloff, the result of thrusting the child into isolated

autonomy is to shatter the newborn's powerful emotional connection with its mother and to cheat its expectations for intimate care. Under these conditions, she wonders if the baby
does not experience its first encounter with life as "hell," a condition of outcast abandonment. Where bodily warmth and loving attention is expected, the child is consigned to isolation. In
contrast to traditional societies that often prolong the babe-in-
arms phase of life well into the first year, our habit in the modern West is to begin forcing the child toward a relationless
self-reliance from the first breath of life. Babies, fresh from the
womb, the most intimate of all relationships, suddenly find
themselves expected to become individuals, like it or not.
Usually they cry in distress until they give up hope. Ego separation begins; isolation becomes the rule that will continue in
force especially for males throughout life.

In dealing here with the drive to achieve a compulsively
masculine power over nature, we have used familiar examples
from contemporary science: splitting the atom, probing the
genome, reshaping the human body or the planet as a whole.
Over the course of the last century, ambitious projects like
this—efforts to gain greater human control over the forces of
nature—have become almost routine. In Mary's time there was
as yet no field of science that could, literally and physically,
exercise such power. The capacity to conquer nature—or at
least convince oneself that conquest is possible—was not yet a
reality. Men had not invented anything more powerful than the
unwieldy, huffing and puffing steam engine, and it was puny in
comparison with lightning and tempest, earthquake and volcanic eruption.

Yet science was all about power. It hungered for the ability
to transform the world. Mary had learned that from Percy,

whose fascination with capturing the forces of nature reached back into his boyhood. This was the intention she prophetically placed at the center of *Frankenstein*, the story of a man who would reconstruct life itself. But when it came to embodying that intention in the narrative of her story, she was at a loss. This is why she gives no description of exactly what Victor Frankenstein might be up to in his laboratory. The best she could do was to offer one macabre chapter filled with blurred, Gothic references to crypts and dissecting rooms, nothing more. Yet she knew in her bones that scientists would not cease until they had achieved the ability to manhandle Mother Nature. So she built her tale around the only images of godlike power available to her: metaphors borrowed from nature itself. She had, after all, dreamed up the story of Frankenstein in Geneva, where portentous power loomed up out of the landscape all around her. The best she could do to depict Victor's overweening arrogance was to give him the Alps for a stage. But she was not the Shelley who first dared to bring these images into art. Rather it was Percy who transformed the heights of Switzerland into a symbol of Promethean aspiration, as if to say "the time has come for men to vie with these mountains." That happened in one moment of blinding inspiration on the day he and Mary made their way into Chamonix and looked up to see Mont Blanc.

5

"The power is there"

The Switzerland Mary knew in 1816 has long since vanished. It lies buried beneath decades of modern industrial culture, much of it—the 747s overhead, the power pylons all around—the creation of the Frankensteinian science she prophesied. The valley of Chamonix, the awesome Mer de Glace, the haughty summit of Mont Blanc—all this was unsullied wilderness when she and Percy came visiting. The area belonged to poor shepherds and peasant farmers, to the ibex and the eagle. Curious travelers were only just beginning to seek out the few ramshackle inns in the area; local herders had but recently begun to hire themselves out as guides for amateur mountaineers.

We have sketches of male tourists from that period challenging the heights in ordinary clothes and shoes, wrapped in mufflers and equipped with nothing more than walking sticks. If there are women with them, they are sometimes shown slipping down the glaciers in their heavy skirts and bustles, holding their hats on their heads as they try to preserve their dignity. Climbing was regarded as a masculine sport. Ladies were advised to watch their men through telescopes from a safe height. There are still foolhardy amateurs today inconveniencing the mountains, though now they usually sport expensive gear. Betty and I watched them setting out by the hour from the lower slopes. Each year several climbing parties are lost to avalanches or must be rescued. The respect people once had for wild things and places is clearly waning as Disneyland fantasies replace natural reality.

It was only after a generation of late eighteenth-century painters and poets had advertised the Alps across Europe as a natural wonder of the world that climbing became popular. A prize was posted for reaching the summit of Mont Blanc. It was claimed in 1786, the first step toward a mountaineering craze that would rapidly grow into a worldwide outdoor sport. More so than big game hunting, mountain climbing, especially in the Swiss Alps, came to be identified with the intoxicating project of "conquering" nature. The great peaks—the Jungfrau, the Matterhorn, the Eiger—were assigned the role of challenging adversaries. This was where (in the words of the poet A. G. Butler) men "warred with Nature, as of old with gods, the Titans."

Today Chamonix is only a few hours away from Geneva by bus. Tourists can "do" the valley in the morning, have a *prix fixe* luncheon, and move on to see several more Alpine peaks before dinner. In their day, Mary and Percy spent two days threading their way along the wild River Arve by foot and on muleback. They had to work cautiously around cataracts and waterfalls and take refuge where they could when the weather turned bad. They arrived "dead with fatigue." But what awaited them at the end of their exhausting trip will never again be seen: the mountain valley, the Mer de Glace, the towering Alps—all still in their pristine majesty. When he caught his first sight of the summits of Chamonix, Percy reported experiencing "a sentiment of ecstatic wonder not unallied to madness."

Now, this lovely country has taken sick with the epidemic blight of tourism. Souvenir shops, hotels, pizza parlors, and tour buses very nearly shoulder the natural beauties out of sight. It requires an artist's imagination not to paint the scene, but to sweep away the commercial clutter that lines the streets. And of course Betty and I were doing Chamonix no favor, crowding in with the others to gawk at the wonders.

But then I was pleased to believe I had a good reason for vexing this magnificent landscape. I was there to try seeing the Alps as Mary had seen them when Frankenstein and his monster were still taking shape in her mind. No easy task these days. The skies above the snowy peaks are constantly congested with hang gliders. They fill the air overhead like some queer, ungainly hybrid of bird and human floating on plastic, multicolored wings: fire red, navy blue, plaid, polka dot, checkered. Unless one gets to the scene early in the day before the gliders arrive, it is all but impossible to gain a clear view of the mountains as they once were. I did the best I could to ignore the gliders as I focused on the question foremost in my mind that day: Why had Mary decided to make Switzerland the location for her still amorphous story?

The answer is not obvious. Few people these days know *Frankenstein* has any connection with Geneva. Most movies choose a more generic Gothic locale: the Black Forest, a wind-swept moor. The characters in the films are more apt to have German than French accents. There is nothing in the plot or characters that requires a Swiss setting. Mary might very well have brought her story home and placed it in the English countryside.

Why Switzerland? The answer, I felt certain, had to do with Percy and with Mont Blanc. It also had a great deal to do with Mother Nature and Father God.

O N HIS WAY to Chamonix, Percy blithely registered himself at hotels along the way as "Percy Bysshe Shelley, Democrat, Great Lover of Mankind, and *Atheist.*" He wrote in Greek, but later that year a fellow Englishman spotted the outrage and reported it to the English press, which promptly took Percy to task for once again flaunting his godlessness.

Though he publicly proclaimed himself a nonbeliever, Percy had no difficulty finding God in nature—and never more vividly than in the presence of Mont Blanc. His response to the great height was little short of an epiphany:

> When I gaze on thee
> I seem as in a trance sublime and strange
> To muse on my own separate fantasy. . . .
> Mont Blanc yet gleams on high—the power is there,
> The still and solemn power of many sights
> And many sounds, and much of life and death.
> . . . The secret strength of things
> Which governs thought, and to the infinite dome
> Of heaven is as a law, inhabits thee!
> And what were thou, and earth, and stars, and sea

> If to the human mind's imaginings
> Silence and solitude were vacancy?

Words like these, a soaring paean to the mountain and all natural beauty, remind us that Romantic artists are the spiritual headwaters of modern environmentalism. The splendor they taught us to see in wilderness still provides the emotional power behind the politics of the movement.

Percy was the most scientifically oriented of all the English Romantics. While still a schoolboy, he had set up his own electrical laboratory where he boldly, often dangerously, experimented on everything in sight, including his sister and the family cat. He relished attending scientific lectures, especially the electricity demonstrations that were then touring Europe. Like many another revolutionary spirit of the Enlightenment, he had pledged his very soul to science as the hope of the future. "The cloud of mind is discharging its collected lightning," he declared. There was no question where he stood in the warfare between science and religion. "For my part I would rather be damned with Plato and Lord Bacon than go to Heaven with Paley and Malthus"—Paley, the rational theologian, and Malthus, the dour economist, being Percy's representatives of intellectual repression.

All very exhilarating. And yet it was Percy's unbridled fascination with the "human mind's imaginings," especially his obsession with seeking out "the secret strength of things," that worried Mary. What was it he most essentially loved about the mountain? It was the image of cold, austere omnipotence. Mary astutely discerned in Percy's lust for knowledge a darker, more troubling note that haunted her all the while she worked at her novel.

The trip the couple took to the Vale of Chamonix to view Mont Blanc was the high point of their journey that summer. It was also the experience that most dramatically sharpened their radically different views of our relations with nature. By the time Percy had finished his hymn to Mont Blanc, he had stamped the Swiss landscape with exactly the identity Mary intuitively knew she needed for her story. In *Mont Blanc*, Percy had elevated raw natural beauty to the sublime, especially as it was displayed in the unruly power of great, wind-swept mountains. *Frankenstein*, a tragedy of man's misguided fascination with power, would have to be a story set in an Alpine wilderness that both mirrors and mocks that ambition.

There is a scene in the 1995 Kenneth Branagh movie *Mary Shelley's Frankenstein* that manages to capture something of what Mary wanted the Alps to represent in her tale. In a dizzyingly panoramic shot, the camera sweeps across the sheer face of the mountains above the Mer de Glace. Only after the eye adjusts to the stupendous scale of the scene do we spy Victor Frankenstein clambering up the immense glacier. He looks like an intrusive insect on the gleaming wall. The ice caves all around seem ready to devour him. That was what Mary wanted as a backdrop for the tale of *Frankenstein*: a sense of overwhelming natural power, the power that tiny Victor so impudently hopes to appropriate. In the film as in the original tale, this is the setting that brings the monster and his maker face to face. It is an impressive and chilling encounter, the moment at which Victor fully realizes he has strayed far out of his depth. All the wild force of untamed nature is in this monstrous creation before him. He has conjured a fiend out of darkness, but he cannot control him.

Ever since the Romantics, mountains have been the most dramatic focus of man's attempt to subjugate nature. Few realize how great a role Percy played in teaching us to admire mountains precisely for their inhuman qualities. In his poetic eye, Mont Blanc was a transcendent entity. The mountain's very ruggedness—"rude, bare, and high, ghastly, and scarred, and riven"—made it all the more awesome, as did its disdainful strangeness. It was "a desert peopled by the storms alone."

In her study of mountains in literature, Marjorie Hope Nicolson credits the Romantics, and especially Percy, with having discovered the "aesthetics of the infinite." In mountains, they saw "palaces of nature," a "throned Eternity in icy walls of cold sublimity" that defied measurement or formula. In the past, European eyes had all but universally seen mountains as ugly piles of jagged rock. There was no symmetry or proportion to them, nothing that could be seized upon by reason. They were just immensely, shapelessly *there.* But mountains and volcanoes were the largest, most violent natural forces the Romantics knew, and the most impenetrable. The painters of the time delighted in depicting the Alps as a world out of balance; they presented colossal boulders teetering on the edge of an abyss or waterfalls carrying away everything before them.

This was not the regularity of Newtonian nature; until the invention of fractal geometry, it escaped mathematical expression. It was something formlessly primeval. Mont Blanc was the very chaos with which God, if there was a God, had wrestled to create the universe. It belonged to the most ancient order of being, before there was light and balance and structure. In Percy's mind, that made Mont Blanc the perfect symbol of

sovereign nature, the source from which all knowledge flows
down and down to the mind of man like a rushing river.

> The everlasting universe of things
> Flows through the mind, and rolls its rapid waves,
> Now dark, now glittering—now reflecting gloom—
> Now lending splendor, where from secret springs
> The source of human thought its tribute brings
> Of waters—.

Power was what Percy loved in Mont Blanc, and power was
what he wanted from the mountain. The word echoes through
every stanza. As in his poem *Prometheus Unbound*, which is
also set in a craggy wilderness, he creates vertiginous scenes
that enhance the magnitude and magnificence of the setting:

> Far, far above, piercing the infinite sky,
> Mont Blanc appears,—still, snowy and serene—
> Its subject mountains their unearthly forms
> Pile around it, ice and rock; broad vales between
> Of frozen floods, unfathomable deeps,
> Blue as the overhanging heaven

Percy's ode to Mont Blanc is riddled with images of soaring
height and violence. The mountain is ensconced in storm,
lightning, thunder, earthquake, gale, tempest, cloud, rainbow.
It is precisely this godlike omnipotence that the poet would
have flow into him. In its presence he becomes yielding, submissive, feminine, as if waiting to be ravished.

> My own, my human mind, which passively
> Now renders and receives fast influencings,
> Holding an unremitting interchange
> With the clear universe of things around.

As an aesthetic, Percy's celebration of mountain landscape opens new territory. But in religious terms, his point of reference is ancient. His infatuation with the holy mountain harks back to a crucial period of cultural warfare, the point in history at which God became *He*. Percy's poem allows us to sense the awe with which men once regarded the powerful phallic imagery of stormy heights. In his imagination, Mont Blanc is elevated to the status of an almighty deity, "remote, serene, and inaccessible." The mountain takes its place among the sky-gods—Zeus, Jupiter, Woden, Varuna—harsh male divinities that were carried across the world by nomadic conquerors. In these patriarchal societies, which invaded Europe in the Bronze Age, the major deities were fierce gods of battle and wrath whose mythic imagery would now undergird the authority of fathers and kings. In his original identity, the god of the Hebrew tribes, the mountain-dwelling Yahweh, hidden by cloud and smoke, was such a divine lawgiver ruling from atop Mount Sinai.

In our day, the women's movement has elaborated these long-forgotten prehistoric upheavals into a quasi-legendary watershed in the evolution of human culture. Many feminists believe, with some scholarly validity, that wherever the sky-god worshippers conquered, relations between the sexes were permanently transformed. Men became the rulers, women their chattels. Men took charge of the world; a woman's place was the kitchen and nursery. From that time forward, all the qualities that make for dominance were stamped as "male." The surviving sign of that change is the cult of sun and sky personified by a divine Lord and Master who rules from above. In turn, the old Earth Mother deities were diminished or replaced. They became, at best, mere consorts to mighty Father Gods. Now god was a king, and the king was god. As the feminist cultural critic Charlene Spretnak sees it, "After the establishment of patriarchal chieftain systems in which warrior cults were central, the Earth was desacralized in favor of a sky-god, and female sexuality, like the larger forces of nature, came to be regarded by men as potentially chaotic, engulfing, and devouring." In some cultures, older female deities were changed into dark, menacing creatures that haunted the unknown regions beyond the civilized city. Catherine Keller calls this a process of "mythological defamation" which would "systematically transmute the images of female power into the monster, the enemy, and the Amazon."

How accurate these historical speculations may be remains to be seen. What feminist psychology has added to this ambitious interpretation of prehistory is the possibility that these mythic transformations continue to shape the lives of modern men and women, and nowhere more consequentially than in the psyche of the scientist. There patriarchy has succeeded in disguising itself as objective truth. "By masculinist epistemology," observes Ellyn Kaschak, "I mean systems of knowledge that take the masculine perspective unself-consciously, as if it were truly universal and objective." Or, as she puts it more succinctly, "masculinity is the only point of view that does not know it is one."

6

мacho science

Percy was too deeply inspired by the storm-swept Alpine vistas he brought home from Geneva to exhaust their inspiration in a single poem. As magnificent a lyric as *Mont Blanc* may be, another, greater hymn to the powers of nature was gestating in his mind all the while he and Mary sojourned among the mountains. The wilderness symbol was destined to reappear a year after *Frankenstein* was published in *Prometheus Unbound*, but now raised to an even higher intensity.

Prometheus Unbound, Percy's celebration of revolutionary politics and humanistic values, has a curious relationship to *Frankenstein.* One scholar calls the two works "alternative life-histories of the same metaphor." They are companion creations, conceived in the same place, at the same time, under much the same circumstances. Between the two there is an interplay that shows us how divergently sexual politics can mold the perceptions of men and women, even when they are lovers. We are left to decide for ourselves: Who had the fuller understanding of Prometheus—Percy or Mary?

Both Mary and Lord Byron played a part in bringing the figure of Prometheus to Percy's attention. At the Villa Diodati, Byron was inspired by the mountain setting to write his own brief Prometheus poem. He chose to praise Prometheus as a rebellious spirit, one whose will is "Triumphant where it dares defy." Byron, who was by now regarded in respectable society across Europe as the devil incarnate, of course saw himself cast in the role of the suffering Titan. When the poem was done, he prevailed upon Mary to copy it out for publication. Both he and Percy used Mary for copy work whenever she was nearby; it was a practice that always put women in their place. (Before the typewriter became a woman's tool, females were expected to have neat handwriting.) Mary did the job cheerfully and may have profited from the assignment. Perhaps it was while she was serving as Byron's dutiful amanuensis that she first encountered the myth that would give *Frankenstein* its striking subtitle: *The Modern Prometheus.* In her remaining days at the villa, with Byron's lines fresh in her thoughts, she may very well have kindled Percy's interest in the myth. Percy knew the story well from the original Aeschylus drama; it was one of his favorite Greek texts. A friendly rival of Byron, he may have felt moved to try his hand at the same subject.

What we can say for certain is that Percy returned from Geneva with two great themes stewing in his imagination. The image of mountains as a symbol of transcendent power; the image of the mutinous Titan chained to a mountain, condemned to suffer eternally in "a ravine of icy rocks." *Prometheus Unbound* brings these images together in a poetic and philosophical marriage. More so than *Mont Blanc, Prometheus Unbound* is a song of the heights, a dizzy rhapsody offered to flight and the transcendence of all limits. In his preface, Percy compares his Prometheus to Milton's Satan and praises both for their "courage, and majesty, and firm and patient opposition to omnipotent force."

All the while Mary was writing *Frankenstein*, Percy was mulling over his masterpiece. We have no records to tell us what passed between the two as they toiled away at these parallel works. Though Percy did not settle in to work at his poem in earnest until he had helped Mary get *Frankenstein* into print, surely they exchanged ideas and insights along the way. I can imagine the heady discourse their overlapping and sharply contrasting interest in the myth of Prometheus may have occasioned. I suspect it would have been for the most part a one-way conversation: Percy talking, Mary listening. Percy was a domineering man to whom Mary readily deferred, keeping her own thoughts more subdued. I can see her swept up in admiration at Percy's adulation of the chained Titan. But while Percy was growing more intoxicated with ideas of Promethean daring, Mary was backing off, growing more prudent. She would have been the first to hear Percy recite from the most intoxicating work of lyric poetry in the English language, words that proclaim the Faustian aspirations of modern man. But Mary was surely not hearing the words in the same spirit in which they were read.

> The lightning is his slave; heaven's utmost deep
> Gives up her stars, and like a flock of sheep
> They pass before his eye, are numbered, and roll on!

The tempest is his steed, he strides the air;
And the abyss shouts from her depth laid bare,
Heaven, hast thou secrets? Man unveils me; I have none.

". . . the lightning is his slave." Mary would have fixed on that image. In *Frankenstein*, the turning point in young Victor's life comes when he sees a tree riven by lightning and blasted to ashes. The boy is entranced by the sight; it grips him with "curiosity and delight." He at once turns to the study of electricity. In the destruction of life, Victor finds the inspiration to create life. Later, when he looks back over his career, he identifies this as his first step toward "evil."

One point seems certain: Percy's deepening fascination with Prometheus surely served to confirm Mary's decision to use her husband as the model for Victor Frankenstein. For Mary, Victor was more than mere fiction. He was patterned on the man she knew and loved best. Scholars have found many parallels between the mad scientist and the lyric poet. The name "Victor" was the pseudonym Percy once used in his youth; Elizabeth, Victor's sister and bride-to-be, was named after Percy's own beloved sister. Victor's interest in the alchemists and in electricity mirrors Percy's youthful pre-occupations. Above all, Victor was given Percy's impulsive fascination with the powers of nature; he harbored the same passionate but heedless desire to harness them for human betterment.

Percy may have been the man who prefigured Victor Frankenstein, but he was deaf to his wife's warning against reckless bravado. In his ode to Prometheus, he betrays no awareness of Mary's appeal for prudence; he is without trepidation. The poet had a daredevil mind. No doubt he would have regarded Mary's reservations as the sort of girlish squeamishness that inhibits the heroic pursuit of knowledge, clear evidence that science is not for women.

ERCY HAD NO DOUBT that Prometheus was "the highest perfection of moral and intellectual nature, impelled by the purest and the truest motives to the best and noblest ends." That is exactly the way Victor Frankenstein regarded himself on the threshold of his great breakthrough. "A new species would bless me as its creator and source," he predicted. "Many happy and excellent natures would owe their being to me. No father could claim the gratitude of his child so completely as I should deserve theirs."

But Mary saw something else in the Titan's daring, a darker possibility. Yes, there was the sincere desire to improve our lives; but linked to that was a domineering impetus, a willingness to endure and to inflict suffering in a great cause and with that a certain arrogance. I suspect she would have understood what Abraham Maslow had in mind when he used the following ordeal from his own medical training to probe the psychology of science.

> The first operation I ever saw was almost a representative example of the effort to desacralize, i.e., to remove the sense of awe, privacy, fear, and shyness before the sacred and of humility before the tremendous. A woman's breast was to be amputated with an electrical scalpel that cut by burning through. As a delicious aroma of grilling steak filled the air, the surgeon made carelessly "cool" and casual remarks about the pattern of his cutting, paying no attention to the

freshmen rushing out in distress, and finally tossing this
object through the air onto the counter where it landed with
a plop. It had changed from a sacred object to a discarded
lump of fat. There were, of course, no tears, prayers, rituals,
or ceremonies of any kind, as there would certainly have
been in most preliterate societies. This was all handled in a
purely technological fashion, emotionless, calm, even with
a slight tinge of swagger.

Maslow had a name for the surgeon's casual demeanor. He
called it "counterphobic toughness." What was the real lesson
the doctor was teaching his students that day? That a good scientist does not flinch in the face of suffering or gore. He
remains detached, cool, objective. His control over nature
begins with control over himself: over disgust, horror, shame,
inhibiting sympathy. Only in that way can he see the world as it
really is, untainted by sentiment or empathy. More than a matter of methodology, objectivity is a matter of character. It
requires unswerving dedication to an ideal. In our popular culture, that ideal has been instructively embodied in the figure of
Mr. Spock, the alien First Science Officer in the popular *Star
Trek* series. Faced with horrors that strike panic in the hearts of
his human colleagues, Mr. Spock never blinks. He merely raises
an eyebrow and murmurs, "Interesting."

Were he a real person, Victor Frankenstein would have
begun his career as a medical doctor. Like Maslow, he would
also have found himself one day being "blooded" by his
instructors. There would have been no female colleagues in
sight, nothing but young men proving their manhood. In his
day the only women allowed near an operating room were
either patients or cadavers. Through the eighteenth century,

men were busily staking out every area of medicine, including gynecology and childbirth, as *theirs*, the exclusive province of masculine competence.

In *Frankenstein* Mary perceptively attributes to young Victor the manly toughness that Maslow was still experiencing in his medical education two centuries later. She credits Victor's father, a man of the Enlightenment, with having raised his son to confront nature free of all "supernatural horrors." Once Victor undertakes his research, the darkness of the tomb, the bodies of the dead hold no fear for him. "My attention," he reports with a certain pride, "was fixed upon every object the most insupportable to the delicacy of the human feelings." He steels himself to dissecting specimens both dead and alive. "I tortured the living animal to animate the lifeless clay," he confesses, and "disturbed with profane fingers the tremendous secrets of the human frame."

Later in the tale, looking back ruefully from the last days of his life, Victor is horrified by his capacity to do the "intolerable." But he recalls that at the time "a resistless and almost frantic impulse urged me forward; I seemed to have lost all soul or sensation but for this one pursuit." Mary, far more so than Percy, was aware of how easily the line can be crossed between Promethean yearnings and macho posturing. The Titan who rises above the inhibitions of ordinary people runs the risk of losing his common humanity, and then all that is left is bravado.

I can still remember my first lesson in macho science. Oddly enough, I learned it from a woman, and a very grandmotherly one at that. Her name was Miss Wells. She was my sixth grade biology teacher. I recall the day she made a jolting announcement. The time had come to kill and dissect Croaker. Croaker was the frog we had been treating as a classroom pet. Kill Croaker! Several of us flinched at the prospect. The girls, most of them at least, hid their eyes, squealing "No! No!" and pled for the poor creature's life. But Miss Wells steeled us to the task. "Now let's see who the good little scientists are," she said. Thus challenged, the boys at once played tough, refusing to "turn green" in front of the girls. Not wanting to seem a sissy, I did the best I could to seem unfeeling.

Miss Wells was an effective recruiter. She had found a way to weed out those who were unsuited for a career in science. Though I did not know it at the time, I was among the unsuited. Ashamed of my unease, I decided biology was not for me. It was my first lesson in the hidden sexual politics of "fitness." Generations before Darwin applied natural selection to evolution in the wild, the survival of the scientifically "fittest" was being decided in the classrooms and laboratories of the Western world. Its purpose was to select certain sensibilities and reject others. Since being tough blends readily with being macho, boys have the advantage. It might almost seem they are born to be "good little scientists."

Macho science has licensed any number of aggressive and unfeeling acts. One could make a long list of horrors, ranging from animal and human experimentation that reaches sadistic extremes to reckless forms of biotechnology that now threaten to derange the germline of our species. All have been justified as a fearless search for knowledge that allowed nothing, no moral quibble, no squeamish sentimentality, to stand in its way. At a certain point, unflinching toughness in the face of high risk and great suffering becomes a philosophical stance in life. Pressed far enough, the drive to prove oneself "tougher-than-thou" becomes a sort of vulgarized Stoicism, the philosophy that has long been associated with atomism. This is the point at which science ceases to be the proud defense of reason and becomes a nihilistic attack upon the meaning of life.

In the ancient world, Stoic philosophers took pride in their ability to face the harshness of life without whimpering. Their basic teaching was straightforward: The world is not a friendly place. It offers little comfort, it does not heed our cries for solace or salvation. It is governed by material forces and natural laws that take no account of our tender human sensibilities. The virtuous man accepts that. He confronts life like a soldier going into battle. One can begin to see scientists gravitating toward this warrior-like role from the mid-eighteenth century on, when atheism became a crusading cause, a principled effort to debunk religion. Stoical resolution became the brave man's way to stand against a godless universe. That was always the philosophical value of atomism: it was the nonbeliever's trump card. It allowed men of reason to assert that only chance governs the world. After all, a universe of mindless particles that simply fall into place in an infinite void would seem to be the ultimate denial of meaning. The historian Carl Becker summarizes the deep pathos of this worldview. "Man," he writes, "is little more than a chance deposit on the surface of the world, carelessly thrown up between two ice ages by the same forces that rust iron and ripen corn."

At the turn of the twentieth century, the great scientific bugaboo was entropy. Entropy, as formulated in the second law of thermodynamics, was used to predict the inevitable "heat death" of the universe, that point at which the last star would cool to ash. Entropy was "time's arrow," and the arrow was headed straight into the dark and all-consuming void. The classic statement of what might be called entropic Stoicism was

Bertrand Russell's *A Free Man's Worship*, written in 1905. "Man," Russell proclaimed, "is a product of causes which had no prevision . . . his origin, his growth, his hopes and fears, his loves and beliefs are but the outcome of accidental collocations of atoms." And yet, though "the temple of man's achievement must inevitably be buried beneath the debris of the universe in ruins," Russell was proudly unafraid. "Only on the foundation of unyielding despair," he insisted, "can the soul's habitation henceforth be safely built."

Nearly a century later we can hear the same melancholy refrain in the words of one of our greatest contemporary physicists, Steven Weinberg. Weinberg laments that nonscientists cannot accept the fact that human life is "just a more-or-less farcical outcome of a chain of accidents reaching back to the first three minutes [after the Big Bang]!"

> It is hard to realize that this all is just a tiny part of an overwhelmingly hostile universe. It is even harder to realize that this present universe has evolved from an unspeakably unfamiliar early condition, and faces a future extinction of endless cold or intolerable heat. The more the universe seems comprehensible, the more it also seems pointless.

For Weinberg, only scientific intellect redeems life from total inanity. "The effort to understand the universe is one of the very few things that lifts human life a little above the level of farce and gives it some of the grace of tragedy."

Macho like this is just as much at home in the life sciences as in physics. In fact, one is now more apt to find biologists staking out the farther reaches of Stoic resignation. Hence the words of the Nobel laureate Jacques Monod: "Man knows at last that he is alone in the universe's unfeeling immensity, out of which he emerged only by chance. His destiny is nowhere spelled out, nor is his duty." Russell's fatalism was based on accidental atoms; as a biologist, Monod preferred to ground his view of life in the genes, which he believed are randomly shuffled in the process of natural selection. But Monod's theme is the same: a call to show courage in the face of "the world's uncaring emptiness."

At times, scientific toughness can reach an absurd extreme. It can be read even into cosmology, the science seemingly most remote from our earthly concerns. For example, an essay from a science journal, titled "Cosmic Cannibals," opens with an ominous pronouncement: "Predatory galaxies are stalking the universe, and our own Milky Way is one of them." If we were dealing with nothing more than metaphors, this would be a revealing way to characterize the cosmos. But some cosmologists have gone beyond metaphors in making their science as macho as possible. One hypothesis formulated by Lee Smolin at the University of Pennsylvania suggests that there is an infinity of competing universes, each the result of a black hole. Therefore, "universes with the most black holes . . . would produce the most 'offspring' and would quickly come to dominate their competitors." This is dog-eat-dog Social Darwinism raised to a cosmic magnitude, a telling example of how pervasively, yet casually, science has become gendered. One cannot even imagine what evidence there could be for a multiplicity of universes. The theory is a speculative fantasy intended to bring the entire universe within a suitably masculine worldview.

There is a terrible irony to these efforts to portray nature as alien, hostile, or meaningless. At the very time that scientific Stoics began to use size in order to prove that the Earth was an insignificant speck in the cosmos and life a meaningless aberration, both physics and biology were undermining the naive concepts of large and small that we learn in childhood. Science was beginning to understand the astonishing amount of physical structure nature can pack into the cellular and sub-atomic realms. No society in history has ever been able to appreciate more fully that small things are not minor things. For some people, these remarkable discoveries might have ranked as miracles; but for the most part, science elected to adopt a Stoic stance. It preferred to atomize, isolate, and toughen.

Is macho science of this kind built into the testosterone of male scientists? *Must* science, as pursued by men, be dominated by a compulsive, adolescent masculinity fashioned from the images of threat and menace? Feminist psychologists do not think so. They have not simply named the separative self; they have explored the developmental dynamics that produce it. They believe that macho science begins in the politics of the family.

In the early years of life, every child must master many talents. Among the most basic is the mastery of its gender role. Boys must learn to be boys, and girls to be girls. The roles are acquired so subtly and at so early an age that we can easily mistake them for inborn predispositions, characteristics that are inherited in the genes. Feminist psychologists are not at all sure about that. They speculate that a succession of powerful emotional transformations takes place within the first few years of life that imprints the sexual stereotypes. Defining gender, they insist, is a family affair.

Here is what feminist psychologists believe happens: The early years of a child's life unfold within a complicated pattern of family relationships called the "pre-Oedipal phase." The resolution of this phase sends boys and girls off toward different gender identities. It is among the most challenging insights of feminist psychology to suggest that the sexual politics that govern this early stage of life within the home have everything to do with the way our culture has come to understand the heights and depths of the cosmos. In most modern families in the Western world, whether extended or nuclear, girls have the initial advantage of being brought into life and raised in the world by a caregiver of their own sex. This early and open access to the mother in the pre-Oedipal stage may somewhat offset the common birthing practice we have noted of removing the newborn from the mother and isolating it in a place apart. In any case, girls, unlike boys, are able to identify with their mothers throughout their lives and so learn to value a more fluid, affiliative relationship. Nancy Chodorow, who has done most to map the dynamics of gender-formation in children, has put the basic fact of the matter succinctly. "Women mother." As she goes on to explain,

> a crucial differentiating experience in male and female development arises out of the fact that women, universally, are largely responsible for early child care and for (at least) later female socialization. . . . The fact that males and females experience this social environment differently as they grow up accounts for the development of basic sex differences in personality. . . . feminine personality comes to define itself in relation and connection to other people more than masculine personality does. (In psychoanalytic terms, women are less individuated than men; they have more flexible ego boundaries.)

Chodorow describes the little girl's identity as being "embedded in social interaction and personal relationships."

With that identity comes a high regard for "nurturance and responsibility." Since girls have traditionally been raised to be mothers, they are expected to remain attentive to the needs of others, and eventually to their own children. Within a patriarchal social order, women are permitted few roles to perform outside the home; until very recently in the industrial societies, they could find little in the way of a career except in jobs that emphasize caring: as teachers, nannies, nurses, social workers.

In contrast, boys are expected to stake out a strong, early claim to masculinity. That means becoming something different from their mothers. In order to assert their manliness, they must never be "momma's boys." Rather, they must establish a sense of distance from the mother, even to the point of becoming her opposite. "A boy," Nancy Chodorow tells us, "is required to engage in a more emphatic individuation and a more defensive firming of experienced ego boundaries." Boys, Catherine Keller adds, "experience themselves as not-female, as opposite to the mother with whom they first identified, and therefore as separate. Their affective and relational capacities are nipped in the bud."

Building such a rigid demarcation that identifies the self as *not* mother, *not* female is no easy matter. Rooting out "the woman in us" requires a terrific act of will. After all, the baby's earliest relationship with the mother must always be to some degree warmly enveloping and engulfing—as when the child feeds at the breast. Freud made something very special of this babe-in-arms interval. He believed it gave rise to an "oceanic feeling" that blurs the boundaries of the self. If the child is not properly reared, Freud warned, this confused state will lead to a sense of "oneness with the universe." He believed that various forms of religious experience derive from this early, fluid sense of identity. It is precisely the function of the "reality principle," as he called it, to prevent such a steady drift toward mystical unity.

In order to rescue his masculinity from this blurred, infantile condition, the boy baby must draw a firm psychological line. Creating this ego boundary is the beginning of the separative self. It is created out of an emotionally driven need to distance oneself from the feminine, and indeed from the entire surrounding universe. Freud, who standardized his psychology on the male ego, puts it this way: "Originally, the ego includes everything; later it separates off an external world from itself. Our present ego-feeling is, therefore, a shrunken residue of a much more inclusive, indeed all-embracing, feeling which corresponded to a once intimate bond between the ego and the world about it."

That "shrunken residue" of the self has, however, managed to make a great deal of history. It is the beginning of the intellectual capacity we call "scientific objectivity," the ability to treat everything in nature as distant, alien, other. Traditionally we regard nature as feminine. Not only as feminine, but as a mother. When little boys are called upon to distance themselves from the femininity they find in their primary caregiver, the ego they create is ideally suited to the scientist's task of distancing himself from the mothering Earth. This ego is then validated by the surrounding male-dominated culture as "normal," as "adult," as our one reliable link with reality.

Object Relations is the post-Freudian school to which many feminist psychiatrists have turned for a more constructive approach to child development. Object Relations theory pays particular attention to the pre-Oedipal period in which children begin to separate themselves from a mother figure that has come to seem all-powerful, especially in societies like our own where breadwinning usually takes the father away from the home. Most Object Relationists believe boys disengage from the mother in ways that leave them emotionally isolated within hard-edged ego boundaries. Growing up to be a manly man entails censoring all traces of femininity within themselves in order to make that separation secure. "The self-identity of the boy child," Marti Kheel observes, "is thus founded upon the negation and objectification of an other."

Pitted against this alienated other, the male grows up to be sharply and competitively differentiated. The result may be more than a matter of personal psychology; it may bleed over into the natural philosophy of the culture. Catherine Keller makes a telling observation:

> It would seem that the sense of self inflicted upon males bears a startling resemblance to the Newtonian atom! It is separate, impenetrable, and only extrinsically and accidentally related to the others it bumps into in its void. . . . The more fully does a male incarnate this sense of separateness, the more efficiently has he conformed to the machine-economy of modern patriarchy.

From the viewpoint of feminist psychology, overcoming the oceanic feeling means repressing the feminine. It means breaking the maternal tie and becoming everything the mother was *not*. Here is how Evelyn Fox Keller connects the psychological and social dynamics of this great identity crisis:

> Our early maternal environment, coupled with the cultural definition of masculine (that which can never appear feminine) and of autonomy (that which can never be compro-

mised by dependency) leads to the association of female with the pleasures and dangers of merging, and of male with the comfort and loneliness of separateness. The boy's internal anxiety about both self and gender is echoed by the more widespread cultural anxiety, thereby encouraging postures of autonomy and masculinity.

In recent years, social psychologists, concerned with the increasing level of violence among adolescent boys, have brought this insight into play. As Dan Kindlon and Michael Thompson observe, "boys not only feel the pressure to appear masculine, but they feel that, in so doing, they must be clearly not feminine—perhaps anti-feminine—and so they constantly and deliberately attack in others and in themselves traits that might possibly be defined as feminine."

Mainstream psychology, which takes autonomous masculinity as its model, sees the boy's rejection of feminity as progress toward normality. "The ideal self," Ellyn Kaschak observes, "is made up of the most desirable qualities of masculinity without acknowledgement of any bias. That is, the mature and well-developed self is considered to be separate from others, consistent within any context, autonomous, and independent." But feminist psychology sees the creation of this ideal male self as the first step toward censoring the capacity for relationship, and so as a step away from our full human consciousness. "If women sustain a more lucid connection with the unconscious from the outset," Catherine Keller observes, "this makes us not less but more conscious. . . . We do not need to become 'masculine' as we mature, but more focussed, more creative, more luminous just as women." Carol Gilligan puts the same point more colorfully: "It all goes back, of course, to

Adam and Eve—a story which shows, among other things, that if you make a woman out of a man, you are bound to get into trouble."

In 1974 the French scholar Françoise d'Eaubonne coined the term "ecofeminism" to underscore a key insight. D'Eaubonne saw a peculiar psychological link between the condition of women in our society and the treatment of the natural world: both were the victims of a warped sexual politics. At about the same time in the United States, Ynestra King helped launch a new movement called "ecological feminism." She too defined its goal in psychological terms as "the return of the repressed: all that has been denigrated and denied to build this hierarchal civilization with its multiple systems of dominance." The common enemy of nature and womankind soon had a name: *patriarchy*, the dominance of men over all things feminine, both the real women of society and the great symbolic woman Mother Nature.

Coming at the same problem from his boyhood experience, the ecological philosopher Paul Shepard made that connection central to his analysis of the environmental crisis. The childhood and adolescence experience of boys, above all their strenuous separation from the mother, lay at the heart of Shepard's critique. He described the males of our society as "ontogenetically [or developmentally] crippled" from infancy. Boys grow from a protracted adolescence into a false adulthood saturated with "juvenile fantasies." At that point, "irrational feelings may be escalated into highsounding reason when thrown up against a seemingly hostile and unfulfilling natural world. The West is a vast testimony to childhood botched to serve its own purposes, where history, masquerading as myth, authorizes men of action to alter the world to match their regressive moods of omnipotence and insecurity."

If feminist psychology is correct, the very conception of scientific "objectivity" as a disciplined withdrawal of sympathy by the knower from the known, is male separation anxiety writ large. Written, in fact, upon the entire universe.

7

The Rape of Nature

In the final stages of working on *The Memoirs of Elizabeth Frankenstein*, I received two memorable comments. Both had to do with gender, the main theme of the novel. One was the strongest single criticism offered by my editor. Soon after I came home from Geneva, she returned the manuscript to me, urging me to do something about Victor. He was, she felt, becoming just too hard to take. "You have made him too stereotypically macho," she insisted. "Men aren't *that* bad!" I took her advice and set to work humanizing the story's central figure. How did I do that? By making him more loving, more caring, more sensitive to Elizabeth's needs. In short, by "feminizing" him a bit more.

But even more striking was the comment I received from another woman, a scientist I sought out for her special personal perspective. She liked the book more than I thought she might, given the fact that it is a story of mad science. In

fact, she praised it highly. But she added a peculiar observation: "I suspect you have more compassion, patience and
understanding when it comes to this woman stuff than I
have. I wonder how you obtained all that insight."

There is a revealing ambiguity to this remark. There
could be no clearer indication that so-called "feminine"
traits ("woman stuff") have nothing to do with anybody's
gender. They are sensibilities that can be manifested (or
repressed) by either men or women. But I was left to wonder
if the fact that these sensibilities seemed more accessible to
me than to her meant that becoming a successful scientist—
and she was surely that—means leaving "woman stuff"
behind. Was this not clear evidence that the feminist psychologists are right in believing professional science has
been saturated with stereotypically masculine traits?

That point was driven home even more dramatically by
one more remark my scientist reader attached to her letter.
She felt that the act of rape that constitutes the climax of my
novel was "a bit silly." Why? Because Elizabeth "took it all
far too seriously."

Now this was jarring. In my story, the rape of Elizabeth,
Victor Frankenstein's fiancée, is meant to symbolize the rape
of the Earth by modern science. How could I not have Elizabeth take that "seriously"? I wanted her voice to sound a cry
of pain that spoke for all the living planet, at least as poig-
nantly as my literary talents permitted. If the point did not
get across to my reader, was that the fault of my writing . . . or
an insensitivity on her part that comes with being a professional scientist? It is, in any case, a curious fact that the word
we use to characterize the worst transgression against nature
we can imagine is a sexual reference, playing upon the com-

monplace horror-story image of woman as victim. In this case, the damsel in distress is Mother Nature.

The first use of "rape of the Earth" appeared in 1939 as the title of a book by an English soil conservationist. Finding the title too suggestive, the American publisher retitled the book *Vanishing Lands*. In the United States, through the 1940s, the word "rape" was rarely used, even in police reports. Women were "attacked" or "molested," never raped. When Jacques Cousteau used the phrase in 1947 to advertise one of his early television documentaries, it was attention-grabbing. Since then the word has been invoked whenever environmentalists reach for vivid language to condemn the abuse of nature. It was, for example, the rhetorical high point of the movie *Jurassic Park*, when the worried mathematician denounces the cloning of dinosaurs as "the rape of nature."

As clichéd as the phrase has become, it is more than a mere metaphor. It invokes humanity's oldest understanding of the natural world: that nature is our mother. Bloody religious battles have been fought around that image; they have left scars upon the landscape of our consciousness that can still twinge with pain. Recently, for example, I received a journal from a Christian evangelical group called Green Cross. Green Cross seeks to encourage environmental awareness and supports many good causes. But it has a more important item on its agenda. It seeks to warn Christians against the heresy of nature worship. Environmentalists, Green Cross believes, are "under the spell of Mother Earth." They have fallen into "the pit of pagan practices." The group's main message is that "this is our Father's World, NOT Mother Earth."

Language like this may seem to be a vestige of bygone sectarian controversy. But beneath the theological surface, the phrase "rape of the Earth" continues to pack great emotional power. When people use it, I suspect they want to speak out against something that seems to be more than merely wasteful destruction. They want words that connote obscenity—even sacrilege. The standard scientific vocabulary offers nothing that will provide that power. So they borrow the only language that will do the job. They grant the Earth her living presence and then infuse their outrage with highly charged sexual overtones. Even if we no longer believe in mother goddesses, for at least as long as the words echo in the air around us, we can pretend we do, the better to give voice to our indignation.

W E THINK OF the phrase "the rape of nature" as a metaphor, a category we reserve for obvious acts of wanton destruction and waste: the pollution of the seas, the slaughter of an endangered species. But the two key words in the phrase stand on different rhetorical levels. "Nature" is obviously a metaphor for "woman"—a revealing historical association in its own right. But "rape" is emphatically *not* metaphorical, not if we understand the meaning of the word as psychologists or rape victims might explain it to us. In a very real sense, the sexual intercourse in which rape culminates obscures the motivation behind the act, which does not seek physical pleasure but social power.

Rape, we have learned, is a specific kind of violation that has only tangentially to do with the sex act that is its consummation. Underlying the act there is a mentality that licenses domination, a lust for power that is anything but metaphorical. If one focuses on the strange gratification that rape delivers, the act reveals itself to be only marginally sexual and by no means limited to the violation of women. At the psychological level, rape stems from a distinct state of mind that is the same whether the victim is a woman or a rainforest. Rape begins by denying the victim her dignity, autonomy, and feeling. Psychologists now call this "objectifying" the victim. When it is another human being who is being so objectified, everybody (except perhaps the rapist) can clearly see the act as a crime. But when we objectify the natural world, turning it into a dead or stupid thing, we have another word for that. Science.

The rape of nature in the modern world began with precisely such a reconceptualization of the natural environment by the imposition of the atomistic paradigm. The key move was to extend atomism so that it applied to the living as well as the dead. The sexual politics underlying that move are easy to overlook. We have long since forgotten that the words for "matter" and "mother" were originally the same. The basic stuff of nature once belonged to the realm of the fecund mother; the Earth was understood to be her body, the source of all life. But modern science has inverted the relationship. In our society, matter is understood to be dead stuff. The original and normal state of the universe is to be dead. Life, in turn, becomes an anomalous puzzle that cannot be "explained" until scientists in laboratories find a way to animate the dead matter that is the normal condition of things. This amounts to saying that life has no "place" in the world until men—the gender that originally dominated the world of science and still does—can create it all by themselves in a laboratory and express it in a formula. Only then will we "understand" what life is. In the words of Victor

Frankenstein: "To examine the causes of life, we must first have recourse to death."

This is the sense in which physics is regarded as fundamental, the "hard" science on which all else stands. The word "fundamental" is literally intended. What is the "fundament" that the universe sits on? Dead matter. And what is dead matter made of? Atoms, or so it was assumed until well into the nineteenth century. And if not atoms as Galileo and Newton once understood them, then something very like them—perhaps a still smaller piece of ultimate physical material.

At CERN, visitors to the Microcosm Science and Technology Exhibition are cautioned about the finality of particles. A handbook for children on display in the lobby shows a cartoon featuring three groups of scientists who speak for different periods. There is an ancient Greek who says, "All things are composed of tiny indivisible grains and a void." There is a group of physicists from 1935 who declare, "All things are composed of protons, neutrons and electrons, and a void." There is a group of contemporary physicists (circa 1995) who announce, "Since protons and neutrons are made of quarks, it can be said that all things are made of quarks and electrons and a void."

And in the years ahead, as super-colliders smash particles into ever smaller pieces, can we expect to see a twenty-first century group added to the cartoon telling us of still deeper dimensions of physical reality? A recent article I have come across cheerily announces that there is "a new quark on the block." Called the "heavy up" and the "heavy down," these may betoken a fourth family of quarks. And why should they be the last? One is reminded of the popular children's story by Dr. Seuss called *On Beyond Zebra*. In the story, the characters discover an infinite alphabet on the far side of Z, letters with exotic names to be used in naming bizarre creatures. Perhaps one day physicists will tell us that the world is made of zxerkgiboos and zseussabits and zlilliputs. Or will they have something much more remarkable to say. ". . . and then we discovered we were going in the wrong direction. It isn't the little-bitty parts that matter after all, but the pattern that knits them together"?

For as long as it made sense to take things apart to see what they were made of, physicists, who were the masters of the atoms, set the standard for what accurate knowledge of nature must look and feel like. The way forward was the way *down*— down into nature's basement, where the atoms moved with clockwork precision in obedience to Newton's numbers. Atomism gave mathematics its foothold in modern science, a welcome introduction of clarity at a time when natural philosophy had become cluttered with folklore, cloudy symbolism, and plain charlatanry. But Newton's colleague Robert Boyle, the founder of modern chemistry, saw another advantage in the corpuscular philosophy: *Power.*

To see the world as a machine shifted the ethical and psychological balance between the knower and the known. The only relationship henceforth permitted was a cold, unfeeling encounter between a superior knower (the scientist) and an inferior known (the object under study). Boyle was among the first who recognized that the withdrawal of sympathy licenses conduct that would not be permissible within an animistic vision of nature. In the following passage, the pronoun "her" should not be taken lightly as a mere linguistic convention for referring to nature. It came as readily to Boyle as the pronoun "He" for the God who had imposed the rule of law on wily Dame Nature. Here metaphor crosses the line into literal truth. Boyle is quite cold-bloodedly planning the rape of the Earth.

The veneration wherewith men are imbued for what they call nature, has been a discouraging impediment to the empire of man over the inferior creatures of God. For many have not only looked upon it as an impossible thing to compass, but as something impious to attempt, the removing of those boundaries which nature seems to have put and settled among her productions; and whilst they look upon her as such a venerable thing, some make a kind of scruple of conscience to endeavour so to emulate her works as to extol them.

"... *a kind of scruple of conscience.*" Boyle meant something like love . . . loyalty . . . or simply minimal respect. Now all were to be cast aside. As if his intention were not clear enough, he spells it out. "There are two very distinct ends that men may propound to themselves in studying natural philosophy. For some men care only to know nature, others . . . to bring nature to be serviceable to their particular ends, whether of health, or riches, or sensual delight."

One wonders what Boyle meant by "sensual delight." The vision of nature he and his scientific colleagues were creating was fast becoming a mathematical abstraction lacking color, odor, texture, and personality. As Boyle viewed her, nature was reduced to "a great . . . pregnant automaton . . . an engine." Where is the delight in this? Perhaps we gain some hint of his real meaning from the highly sexualized terms that appear so frequently in his work and throughout the science writing of the seventeenth century. The task of the natural philosopher, we are told, is to "probe," "penetrate," and "pierce" nature in all her "mysterious," "secret," and "intimate recesses." Today we take our privileged control over nature so much for granted that we no longer hear the twisted eroticism—the rapacity, the masculine bravado, the heedless arrogance—these metaphors reveal.

It might seem strange that Boyle, writing in a Christian society that had long since banished paganism, should be worried that anybody might see nature as "a venerable thing." Were there those who still honored the old Earth Mother? There were. In particular, there was one surviving school of thought that still retained strong pagan overtones, a sprawling, luxuriant, and nebulous body of thought called "alchemy." Alchemy was in its last days in Boyle's time, but it still had its serious and dilettante practitioners. Historians now estimate that Isaac Newton himself spent more time puzzling over alchemical manuals than he did working on physical experiments. Alchemy evolved out of a very different sensibility. It continued to posit a feminine nature which was referred to as the *Anima Mundi*—the female soul of the world. In Boyle's view, that made the alchemists serious rivals to true science. So he warned against them.

And they, in turn, warned against his science. Boyle had a contemporary who plainly saw where the mechanical philosophy was heading. In one of his metaphysical poems, Henry Vaughan, who knew the alchemical tradition well, puts this guilty confession in the mouth of an unnamed scientist:

> I summoned nature; pierced through all her store
> Broke up some seals, which none had touched before;
> Her womb, her bosom, and the head,
> Where all her secrets lay a-bed.
> I rifled quite; and having passed
> Through all the creatures, came at last
> To search myself . . . .

In adopting atomistic reductionism as its worldview, physics moved to the forefront of the sciences for the next two centuries. In contrast, biology was seen as immature. Until well into the nineteenth century, biology was still being pursued as "natural history," a gentleman's avocation that might take the form of watching birds, catching butterflies, or breeding flowers. By the very character of what they studied, biologists seemed confined to those features of the world that Galileo had labeled "secondary": the lively but illusory realm of the senses where color and smell, shape and texture made the difference. Where qualities like these still mattered, the most one could do was to collect specimens of flora and fauna, catalogue them, and perhaps admire them.

With the invention of the microscope in the seventeenth century, science discovered an astonishing menagerie of microcosmic life. But what the peering eye found beneath the lens was nothing like atoms; rather it was a slippery chaos of cavorting organisms. Biology might be the study of physical nature, but the physicality it studied had none of the supposedly clear definition and mechanical precision of the nonliving world. No hard edges, no mechanical regularity. Compared with the pristine simplicity of physics, biologists seemed condemned to work among mysterious vital forces and life energies. Theirs was a soft science, because what it studied was literally soft, the quivering "jellyware" of life, as some might call it today. There might be atoms somewhere underneath the jelly, but they were buried deep down and hopelessly layered over by pulpy and squishy ephemera.

At least that was how biology was seen until the crusading atomistic mind went to work in earnest upon the living stuff of the world. In the early nineteenth century, at about the same

time Dalton outlined his atomic theory of chemistry, Theodor
Schwann identified the cell as the basic unit of life. Soon after,
cellular chemistry was found to be no different in kind than the
chemistry of the mineral world. By the mid-nineteenth century,
references to vital spirits and organic energies were dropping
from the biological vocabulary. Only a few schools of
thought—*Naturphilosophie* in Germany, Vitalism in France—
dared to hold out, claiming some special, quasi-supernatural
status for life in the universe. The Vitalists' best argument was
their negative critique; namely, that the biochemists of that day
were nowhere near explaining all the intricacies of life. After
all, if life were no more than the sum of its chemical parts, why
could it not simply be concocted in a test tube? The Vitalists
had a point. But the way in which they expressed their reasonable doubts was almost deliberately designed to infuriate hard
scientists. The vital principle was radically elusive, a ghostly
presence that left no trace the eye could find. Vitalism seemed
to be imposing a limit on knowledge. For the modern
Prometheus, such words smack of cowardice or obfuscation.
Most scientists find the very notion of "forbidden knowledge"
provocative.

By the late nineteenth century, biologists were referring to
the cell as a "living atom," eagerly hoping that biology now had
a particle that was as firm, final, and mathematical as anything
to be found in physics. The cell had even entered popular culture as the basic physical unit of life. Gilbert and Sullivan put it
to music in *The Mikado*, whose central character claimed he
could trace his ancestry back "to a protoplasmal primordial
atomic globule." In textbooks of that period, the cell took on a
signature simplicity. It was a line (seemingly of no thickness)
called the "membrane" surrounding a dot (with nothing of

importance inside it) sometimes called the "kernel," but more often the "nucleus"—the same word that would soon be used for the inner structure of the atom. In between the line and the dot there was virtually nothing at all—except a fluid called "protoplasm." Here was how one authority put it, offering as full a description of life as it was understood in the latter nineteenth century:

> For the idea of a morphological cell, one requires a more or less soft substance, primitively approaching a sphere in shape and containing a central body called a kernel. The cell-substance often hardens to a more or less independent boundary-layer or membrane, and the cell then resolves itself according to the terminology of scholars into membrane, cell-contents, and kernel.

It was just that simple. Now all one had to do was position the whole of biology atop that cellular foundation in the same way the physicists had built the universe atop the atom. As Alfred North Whitehead, writing in 1925, observed, "The living cell is to biology what the electron and the proton are to physics." Because of the cell, as Whitehead put it, "biology [now] apes the manner of physics. It is orthodox to hold that there is nothing in biology but what is physical mechanism under somewhat complex circumstances."

What one sees at work in the history of cellular biology is the same eager desire one finds in physics to atomize, isolate, and assign hard boundaries. "These new units," as the historians of science Stephen Toulmin and June Goodfield observe, "could redress the philosophical balance upset by the inert, immutable particles of Newton's physics and Dalton's chemistry." At last biology was in a position to free itself of "physics envy."

But the analogy between the cell and the atom was still rough and inexact. True enough, cells are more empirically *there* than vital spirits; they can be weighed and counted and chemically analyzed. But they look for all the world like purposeful little entities working hard to earn a living. They do not show up as numb, dumb *things* that fit into formulas and move in obedience to strict laws. Biology would not be definitively atomized until the 1950s. Then, like the quark within the proton, the gene was isolated within the cellular nucleus. Now at last, biology had a reasonably good parallel to the fundamental particle. As the hard, isolated core of living tissue, the gene, which has been called "an atom of heredity," had the one characteristic science treasures most highly: It can be acted upon by chance. It is unpredictably shuffled about in the act of procreation, it can be randomly mutated by radiation; it is the object of accident in the same way that the atom was understood to be as it knocked about in the void. The gene conclusively provided Darwin's theory with the randomness it needed to become hard science. Reduced to the statistical permutations of genes, life became "nothing but" the marriage of chance and selection.

As applied to life, the phrase "nothing but" is the rhetorical analog of physical rape. It devalues and makes vulnerable that which is about to be violated by objectifying it. Rape, as Susan Brownmiller reminds us, "is nothing more or less than a conscious process of intimidation by which *all men* keep *all women* in a state of fear." If it provides "sensual delight," to use Boyle's terms, the pleasure arises from the need to prove one's ability to dominate; an act of will, not wantonness. If necessary the rapist destroys his victim in order to have his way. One authority on the subject calls rape a "pseudosexual act." For the rapist, "sexuality becomes a means of compensating for underlying feelings of inadequacy and serves to express issues of mastery, strength, control, authority, identity, and capability." His goal is "to capture and control his victim."

This is the point at which the "rape of nature" ceases to be a metaphor. It is an accurate depiction of a certain psychological mode that predictably produces a certain kind of behavior. In this context, rape stems from a compulsive need to control, to control completely. That need stems from the rapist's sense of inadequacy in the presence of a woman. From that inadequacy flow fear, anger, the need to punish and subjugate. In the personal act of rape, the rapist is angry because he feels insecure. So he must resort to intimidation and violence to control the situation. The same motivation can exist between men and the natural world: fear born of a sensed inadequacy or inferiority. In both cases, the objective is the same: to dominate this elusive, troubling female so that she will do what she is ordered to do. Basically, that requires the objectification of the other; she must become what he wants her to become. She must be stamped with her master's image.

Entitlement is the basis of standard, "normal" male sexuality. Until very recent times—that is, until women asserted the right to control their own bodies—the male was entitled to sexualize the female's body; to judge it, comment upon it, choose it, excite it, take pleasure from it, and give it all the pleasure it was supposed to expect. And where that entitlement was resisted, the male felt licensed to take it by force. It is only within the last few generations that a husband could be found guilty of raping an unwilling wife.

"The rapist," Ellyn Kaschak observes, "is a powerful masculine figure. If masculinist culture defines male sexuality in terms of power, then power is built into male sexuality. So is entitlement." Claiming entitlement, more than seeking sexual pleasure, is the basis of rape. And entitlement means: "I do not ask. I take and do not say thanks."

That same sense of entitlement has come to govern our relationship with the natural world. In four centuries of taking wealth and comfort from the body of the Earth, modern science has not troubled to produce a single rite or ritual, not even a minor prayer, that asks pardon or gives thanks. But then what sense would it make to ask anything of a dead body?

8
"The corpse of my dead mother. . ."

Our hotel in Ferney is a favorite residence for visiting physicists who come from around the world to use the CERN accelerator. Mornings, Betty and I could overhear them in the breakfast room talking about experiments and exchanging notes as they scratched formulas on the table napkins. The conversations were all very crisp and businesslike, matters of budgets, grants, deadlines, schedules, and lots of talk about travel and tickets. At times the conversations seemed almost entrepreneurial. But then these were high-powered professionals in the midst of bustling careers. "I'm due in Tokyo on Monday," I heard one American at a nearby table remark, "so we've really got to get this project wrapped up by the weekend. After that the L3 team moves in. They've been getting a lot of good results." The L3 Collaboration, as I learned later, was made up of a few hundred members from universities around the world. CERN tries to keep its large research contingents international and cooperative, in contrast to some labs, which pit teams of physicists against one another with a reward for the group that achieves a certain result first.

I wondered how many of these busy physicists realized that CERN's status as a scientific Mecca dates back over two centuries. For the better part of a generation in the mid-eighteenth century, this little village was the home of Voltaire, the greatest mind of the Enlightenment. The physicists at CERN have a lot to thank Voltaire for. He was one of the great promoters of science and scientists. His handsome chateau, which he never finished improving, was the intellectual crossroads of Europe. Everybody who was anybody stopped to have a conversation with the Patriarch of Ferney. The very location of his estate tells a story. Voltaire was so controversial a figure that he might at any moment have to flee the French authorities. This was, after all, the time of the repressive *ancien regime*, in whose eyes Voltaire, the voice of reason, was regarded as the enemy of church and state. So he built his home as close to the French-Swiss border as possible, the better to make a quick escape.

Voltaire was a man of many books, but his most famous contribution to the culture of the Enlightenment was his *Éléments de la Philosophie de Newton*, a popularized account of Newtonian physics and the liberating worldview that went with it. His book was among the most widely read of the age. How fitting that his home, once a hotbed of revolutionary ideals, should stand at the entrance to one of the great international scientific centers. Just as the liveliest minds of Voltaire's day made the pilgrimage to Ferney (now renamed Ferney-Voltaire) to encounter the leading ideas of their age, so the most adventurous scientific minds of our time come to CERN in the same spirit, hoping to extend the frontiers of natural philosophy still farther. I think Voltaire would have applauded what the physicists at CERN are up to. He would have seen their work as part of the program of unending progress to which he dedicated his life. If he were around today, he might even have written a sequel to his study of Newton: *Elements of Quantum Philosophy.* No doubt it would also be a bestseller.

Betty and I spent a morning visiting Voltaire's gracious neoclassical chateau, which still dominates the town, and then took a short taxi ride to CERN. Though we could not visit the accelerator itself, we did schedule an afternoon at The Microcosm, CERN's exhibition hall. The Microcosm is a model of popular science. The exhibits are ingeniously designed to make the most advanced ideas in high-energy physics accessible to nonscientists. Many are cleverly inter-active. But what drew my attention immediately was some-thing wholly unexpected. It was a graphic device inlaid in the floor of the exhibition hall: the figure of a giant serpent circling around to swallow its own tail. The image had been given an imaginative meaning. As its caption explained, the universe, like the serpent in the graphic, has come round to know itself in the form of human consciousness. And there laid out around the figure were the major eras of cosmic evo-lution leading up to an image of Rodin's *Thinker.*

How surprising it was to find this quaint image at CERN. Did those who put it there know that it was an ancient alchemical symbol? Alchemists knew the coiled serpent as

Uroboros. In their eyes, it represented the highest goal of their quest: the harmonious union of all opposites, especially the masculine and the feminine sides of the personality. The motto that usually accompanied it was "From the One to the One."

Since we visited CERN, The Microcosm has been renovated and Uroboros has been removed. The Microcosm's designers may never have known its occult meaning, but they had put it to good use nonetheless. Here was the old tail-biter expressing our growing appreciation of the unity that connects the evolution of the cosmos with the human mind. I could not help but believe that Mary would have been gratified to find this remnant of the alchemical tradition at one of the most dynamic centers of modern scientific research. She had, after all, hidden an alchemical subtext in the story of *Frankenstein*. It lay at the core of her moral vision.

VICTOR FRANKENSTEIN BEGINS his study of nature as an alchemist, a tradition that was all but defunct when Mary was writing at the dawn of the machine age. But like all true Romantics, both she and Percy were fascinated by dark and exotic lore. Mary recognized that alchemy was a deeply feminized approach to nature. Traditionally, the "chymical philosophy" was practiced by a male adept in close company with a female consort, the *soror mystica* or mystic sister. The presence of the *soror* may explain the overt sexual imagery that threads through alchemical iconography. The tradition is filled with pictures of coupling partners: kings and queens, gods and goddesses, brides and bridegrooms, and occasionally incestuous siblings. There may have been a sexual yoga concealed behind this erotic male-female symbolism, veiled practices borrowed from Far Eastern sources. Though the *soror* usually appears quite chaste, there are some depictions of her that border on the pulchritudinous, much in the spirit of the Tantric Devadessi, the "god's wife." In any case, in the actual pursuit of the Great Work, the mystic sister was always there to supply those womanly qualities the male sage was bound to need.

There are hints of all this in *Frankenstein*. One of the keys to the story is Victor's lifelong love for Elizabeth, his adopted sister. Elizabeth is surrounded in the story by images of gold, the alchemical symbol of enlightenment. In his early years, Victor, recognizing the need for his feminine half, cleaves to Elizabeth, valuing in her the qualities he cannot find in himself.

Elizabeth is the sensitive, poetic spirit who reminds Victor of the beauty and sanctity of the world. For her, contemplation is enough. Mary tells us how Elizabeth "busied herself with following the aerial creations of the poets, and in the majestic and wondrous scenes which surrounded our Swiss home . . . she found ample scope for admiration and delight." All the while, the more aggressively inquisitive Victor, not satisfied with "the magnificent appearances of things," devotes himself to "investigating their causes." As Victor puts it, "the world to me was a secret which I desired to divine."

It is only after Victor goes off to the university at Ingolstadt that he abandons alchemy. His departure follows immediately upon his mother's death. As if roughly dismissing the women in his life, he unaccountably decides to postpone the marriage with Elizabeth that his mother had so ardently wanted. Indeed, as if to underscore the symbolic meaning of Victor's romance with Elizabeth, throughout the story Mary uses the word "union" for marriage—the term alchemists used to designate the "chymical marriage" of male and female, the highest goal of their work.

At school, Victor's professors scoff at his alchemical studies, calling all he has learned "an exploded system." Mary lends the professors a distinctly demonic character, as if they are sly tempters out to steal Victor's soul. They teach him the New Philosophy, and with it the desire to master and control the elements by brute force. Victor realizes that alchemy has been left far behind. Science now performs "miracles" that the old alchemical teachers could not so much as imagine. His professors invite him to join a new breed of philosopher, those who "penetrate into the recesses of nature and show how she works in her hiding places." These "modern masters," they tell him, "have acquired new and almost unlimited powers; they can command the thunders of heaven, mimic the earthquake, and even mock the invisible world with its own shadows."

Victor is intoxicated by the prospect that has been opened to him. But he is also troubled. He feels that "his internal being" is "in a state of insurrection and turmoil." "I felt as if my soul were grappling with a palpable enemy." But at last he succumbs to the temptation. At which point, Mary gives him a fateful credo. "So much has been done, exclaimed the soul of Frankenstein—more, far more will I achieve; treading in the steps already marked, I will pioneer a new way, explore unknown powers, and unfold to the world the deepest mysteries of creation."

What better image could Mary have found to underscore Victor's reckless passion than to have him create a child without a woman? And what could that child be but a monster, unloved, unwanted, rejected from its birth as an ugly mistake?

That act of rejection was in fact the first image of the story to come to life in Mary's imagination. She claimed that it was visited upon her in a waking dream. The Romantics welcomed such non-normal states of consciousness, regarding them as the gateway to inspiration. Seeking to be ravished by the free imagination, they were the first artists, of the modern period at least, to undertake the deliberate derangement of the sensibilities. At Villa Diodati, both Percy and Byron were dosing on laudanum, heavily enough to give Percy nightmares. Mary apparently needed no narcotic aid. "Acute mental vision," as she calls it, was enough to midwife the creative act. Or at least that is how she remembered the occasion, looking back to the summer of 1816 some fifteen years later.

On the night *Frankenstein* first emerged in Mary's imagination, she had spent the evening silently attentive while Byron and Percy speculated darkly about raising the dead. "When I placed my head upon the pillow," she tells us, "I did not sleep, neither could I be said to think. My imagination, unbidden, possessed and guided me, gifting the successive images that arose in my mind with a vividness far beyond the usual bounds of reverie." The passivity with which she greeted the experience is typical of her capacity for self-effacement. When we arrive at the critical moment in her narrative, the point at which Victor at last sees the monster he has created, Mary allows her mad doctor to lapse into a similarly submissive reverie. He dreams the wildest and most prophetic of dreams. In the unconscious mind whose existence he has so long repressed, the man of reason finds the meaning of his deed.

In nearly thirty years of teaching *Frankenstein*, I have discovered that nothing disappoints students more about the story than the abrupt way in which Mary handles the creation scene. In every film version of the story, this is the moment for big, startling effects. But in Mary's novel, there is nothing. Or rather the creation takes place in the silence between two chapters. And then, simply, suddenly, *it's alive.* Victor gazes in horror at what he has done and then does something that never fails to baffle readers. He flees. He abandons his laboratory and retires to his bedchamber to sleep.

In the 1831 edition of *Frankenstein,* the edition that Mary was given the chance to supervise, this was the moment she chose to illustrate with the frontispiece of the book. There we see the horrified doctor in desperate flight as his creation, wide-eyed with astonishment, comes to life. At just that point, Mary, working with deft psychological intuition, submerges her mad scientist in the unconscious. He sleeps; he dreams. And this is what he dreams:

> Unable to endure the aspect of the being I had created, I rushed out of the room and continued a long time traversing my bedchamber, unable to compose my mind to sleep. At length lassitude succeeded to the tumult I had before endured; and I threw myself on the bed in my clothes, endeavoring to seek a few moments of forgetfulness. But it was in vain: I slept, indeed, but I was disturbed by the wildest dreams. I thought I saw Elizabeth, in the bloom of health, walking in the streets of Ingolstadt. Delighted and surprised, I embraced her; but as I imprinted the first kiss on her lips, they became livid with the hue of death; her features appeared to change, and I thought that I held the corpse of my dead mother in my arms; a shroud enveloped her form, and I saw the graveworms crawling in the folds of the flannel. I started from my sleep with horror; a cold dew covered my forehead, my teeth chattered, and every limb

became convulsed: when, by the dim and yellow light of the
moon, as it forced its way through the window shutters,
I beheld the wretch, the miserable monster whom I had
created.

No special effects. No laboratory. No thunder and lightning.
Instead, the scientific soul laid bare.

Who is the dead mother that history's first mad scientist
holds so pathetically in his arms? Is this not the corpse of
Mother Nature, murdered by his own hands? And who is the
bride whose lips turn cold at his kiss? Is this not his own feminine self? And when the scientist awakens, what has taken their
place in his life? The monster who leers through the curtain
and who will lead him to his own destruction.

Powerful insights for a girl of nineteen. Mary is our best
example of the Romantic imagination finding its way to truth.
A novice writer, she was working far beyond her own powers in
creating Victor Frankenstein's tragic dream. But then perhaps
that is how myths are born, out of the liberated unconscious of
a sensitive soul.

If the feminist psychologists are right, science need not be
ruled by the style and sensibility of the patriarchal ego, because
men themselves need not be. All about us we see men and
women throwing off their stereotypic roles, refusing to be the
slaves of assigned identities. I suspect this transformation of
consciousness has contributed as much to our growing appreciation of complexity, pattern, and system as any experimental
device. As we dignify the feminine in those we live among and
in ourselves, we see the reality of the self-in-relation, the key
category of feminist psychology. And in turn we recognize our
depth of relationship in nature.

9

Deep community

Even today people associate Switzerland with the cuckoo clock, a clever novelty that can be found on display in tourist shops throughout the country. But in Mary's time, the clocks of Switzerland were hardly seen as toys. They were the leading edge of an exciting new technology. Gifted Swiss clockmakers found ways to achieve near miracles with their gears and rachets and springs. They fabricated windup imitations of living things, ingenious automata that could dance and sing, write messages and cipher—or at least mimic doing so. In effect, they had invented the prototype of the computer. The greatest of the Genevan watchmakers, Jacques Vaucanson, found ways to imitate the very metabolism of a real animal. He fashioned a mechanical duck that could eat, digest, and defecate. It toured Europe and was universally proclaimed one of the wonders of the age: clear proof that the mysteries of the living organism would soon be explained.

The museums of Switzerland display these clockwork marvels proudly. I sought them out wherever I could, especially those at the *Musée de l'Horlogerie*, where one can see pocket watches that kept track of the moon, the seasons, and the precession of the zodiac. But music boxes with animated animals were the favorite of the period. The museum's guidebook associates the exhibitions on display with Frankenstein's monster. Mary never mentions it in her story, but there is a connection between the automata of Switzerland and Victor Frankenstein's quest for artificial life, a secret Genevan continuity. Victor, of course, goes about his Promethean task by stitching together putrefying flesh and bone, the macabre remnants of the charnel house and the dissecting theater. As ghastly as these now-familiar Frankensteinian horrors may be, there was something even more chilling about the exquisitely crafted little automata I saw at the *Musée de l'Horlogerie*. The very innocence of their toylike appearance makes them frightening—or at least so I found when I realized that the brightest minds of an enlightened age believed these automata contained the secret of life. That is the same grotesque exaggeration that I find frightening in the contemporary fascination with artificial intelligence. Can those who believe the computer is "an embodiment of mind" really not tell the difference between so poor a caricature and the true original?

Of all the science fiction variations on Mary's monster, perhaps none is more chilling than HAL, the rebellious computer in Stanley Kubrick's film *2001: A Space Odyssey*. Precisely because HAL is disembodied, there is no ugly physique to distract us. We get to the heart of the horror, which does not stem from the machine, but from one's fellow humans who, having lost touch with their own powers of mind and vitality, empower the machines to overstep their limit.

The clockwork toys of Mary's day are now two centuries behind us, but mainstream science continues to be haunted by the possibility that life and mind can be reduced to programmed mechanisms. There are, however, signs of change.

RAPE BEGINS IN the mind of the rapist. He must first deliberately blind himself to his victim's true identity, because to know her for all she is would be to feel her suffering. So the victim must be transformed into an object, a blank, depersonalized screen onto which the rapist projects whatever role he would have her play: virgin, slut, whore, plaything. The final violation is of the body; but the first is of the person.

These days, there are therapeutic techniques that seek to encourage the rapist's sympathy for his victim, group sessions, usually conducted in prison, that try to elicit remorse and pity. The rapist may be required to confront his victim, to feel the lash of her indignity, to admit the harm he has done to her physically and emotionally, above all to face her as a whole and authentic person to whom he bears an ethical obligation. Something like that is spontaneously happening in our relations with the natural environment, not as a confessional revelation, but as a moral awakening. The environmental movement has been the main voice of that awakening, summoning us to a more biocentric view of our place in nature. But underlying this growing ecological awareness is a great sea-change in the sciences. There is a sense of continuity, if not kinship, growing up between ourselves and the nature we have for so long regarded the way Victor Frankenstein regarded his monster: an alien being that is "ours" to do with as we please. No single discovery is responsible for this awakening. There is instead an unfolding frontier of insight and sympathy that appears in the professional literature as a steady stream of new findings, new theories, new paradigms. If there is any one concept that embraces all these changes, it is *complexity.*

Complexity can be highly technical; it has generated whole new schools of mathematics called Chaos Theory and fractal geometry. But from the nonscientist's point of view, these developments can be put quite simply. We can no longer assume that there is some floor to the world of knowledge, a final level of analysis where everything comes down to something as simple as the atom was once thought to be. Reductionism may have finally reached the point of diminishing returns.

Science, in its broad outline, can be divided into three parts: the study of the vast, the study of the tiny, and the study of life which, at least on this one planet, acts as audience to both the vast and the tiny. At all three levels, we see a new master paradigm taking shape before our eyes. Again and again, wherever scientists look, they are faced with the intricate *relatedness* of things. So they find themselves spontaneously employing metaphors of community and communication. Let us briefly consider each of these levels, with an eye not so much for technicalities, but for the imagery and rhetoric that now guide the mind in its search for truth.

1. *The vast.* As recently as the beginning of this century, the universe at large was thought to be no more than an endless void filled with aimlessly drifting atoms. In all eternity, the only development that made the infinity of space interesting was the

purely accidental accumulation of atoms first into stars and then into the planets of the one solar system we know. In all cases, the celestial bodies were seen as no more than dead matter passively drawn into clumps by the force of gravity. The vastness of space enveloping our planet was taken as *prima facie* evidence that life was a meaningless and marginal accident in the alien emptiness. Faced with so inhuman and unfeeling a universe, people spoke of being "strangers and afraid, in a world I never made."

In the course of my lifetime, I have seen all this change. For one thing—and it is the most dramatic change of all—we now know that the universe had a beginning. Since that beginning, it has undergone an historical process of form-building that we call "evolution," a term once reserved for the life sciences. That process intimately connects life to the structure of the stars and galaxies at large. By the process of nucleosynthesis, all the elements heavier than hydrogen and helium, including the carbon that makes our flesh and the iron that runs in our blood, were forged in fiery stellar furnaces and then scattered into space by exploding supernovas like the seeds of life. That process tells us something important about the size of the universe. The cosmos is as big as it is as a result of its evolving structure. It is best understood not as intimidatingly vast, but exactly the right size to make life possible. Only in a universe of a certain temperature and physical stability could life emerge. In the history of time, all these factors—age, size, temperature, and structure—have evolved together. The philosopher Edward MacKinnon has described the universe within this emerging vision as being "nested hierarchies of evolving structures." *Nested . . . hierarchies . . . evolving . . . structures . . .* Every word resonates with significant, new implications.

The number of contingent factors that had to come together to produce those emergent hierarchies—the "cosmic coincidences," so called—has encouraged some scientists to look for explanations that go well beyond dumb luck. Even Fred Hoyle, as hard-headed as any of our leading astronomers, was inclined to believe that "somebody has been monkeying around" with the universe, as he quaintly put it. Such frank astonishment is refreshing in a man of his authority. But of course few scientists are willing to reach for explanations that involve conscious design in nature. The agnostic protocol of cosmology requires them to say that the primordial structuring of the cosmos was due to random "clumps" or "blips" in the original radiation left over from the Big Bang. For reasons unknown, soon after the beginning of time, matter became "uneven" or "imperfect," and presto! by pure chance, the galaxies were born. Or perhaps, as another cosmological theory would have it, there is actually an infinity of universes among which only this one has by sheer accident produced the initial conditions for life and mind. It now requires such artful speculation to maintain an orthodox faith in chance. Skeptics, it would seem, are willing to believe anything.

Despite these desperate efforts to assert the omnipotence of the accidental, in a sense that is both poetic and astronomically accurate, we can now say that the entire cosmos has mothered the living Earth into existence. Thus, the theoretical biologist Stuart Kauffman, a leading figure at the Santa Fe Institute which was founded to study the laws of complexity, tells us that, by way of our deepening understanding of complexity, "we are at home in the universe in ways we have not known since we knew too little to know to doubt. . . . We are all part of this process, created by it, creating it." The astrophysicist Hubert

Reeves puts the same point more lyrically: "we belong to this universe, we are the child of this universe, we are made out of stardust."

2. *The tiny.* Meanwhile, at the atomic level, where the universe was once understood to be even more devoid of meaning—a vacuum filled with nothing but gyrating balls of matter—we have discovered a physical architecture no less complex than that of the great galactic clusters. Within split-seconds of the inflationary process that created the universe, wildly chaotic energy congealed into systems of quarks and leptons so subtle and yet so durable that, in time, the great wheeling galaxies and the intricate chemistry of living things could be crafted from them. Physicists tell us that quarks reside in families that are so tightly knit that they may never let their members roam free as lone individuals. Indeed, the complexity of patterned wholes at the atomic and subatomic level is turning out to be more tenacious, more resistant to disruption than anything built from them. It is almost as if nature were trying to tell us that relatedness is what came first and can never be meaningfully reduced to something more fundamental.

As we have seen, the integrity of the subatomic systems under study at laboratories like CERN is so great and so primordial that physicists frequently cannot blast these systems apart for more than trillionths of a second. When we do so, we are creating a condition that may never have existed except at the bidding of experimental physicists. And even then, as in the case of the exotic meson that has been blasted out of its organized whole by 18 billion electron volts of energy, we cannot be sure we have gotten to the bottom of things. The philosopher of science, Henry Stapp, has aptly characterized the stubborn intricacy of the quantum domain in words that might have been used to describe an ecosystem. "Each atom turns out to be nothing but the potentialities in the behavior pattern of others. What we find, therefore, are not elementary space-time realities, but rather *a web of relationships* in which no part can stand alone; every part derives its meaning and existence only from its place within the whole."

3. *Life.* Finally, at the biological level between the vast and the tiny where complexity studies began, we are discovering patterns within patterns within patterns, none of which can be sensibly reduced to the behavior of isolated parts or competitive agents. Not only is this true of the organs and structures of living things, but it has proven to be a central theme of the entire evolutionary story. In what may be the greatest biological breakthrough since Darwin, Lynn Margulis has shown that multicellular life is made up of "composite organisms" that arise from "the concerted capacities of millions of microbes that evolved symbiotically to become the human brain." This means that communal reciprocity may have been a leading force in shaping the course of evolution from microbes to the mind. When Margulis first proposed her theory, it was considered ludicrously far-fetched. She dared to refer to cells, once regarded as the atomistic elements of biology, as "microbial collectives" and "bacterial confederacies." In the process of evolution, she held, "they cooperated and centralized, and in doing so formed a new kind of cellular government."

Margulis has since been vindicated. It is now widely accepted that we are, as she puts it, "products of symbiosis over billions of years . . . a symbiotic alliance that becomes permanent." Within this new "autopoietic" (self-sustaining) vision of life on Earth, biologists are more and more adopting images of harmonious relationship. For example, the cellular membrane was once called a "wall" because it was at first taken to be a solid barrier that passively confined an undifferentiated blob of protoplasm. But the wall became a system, and the textbooks now describe it as a dynamic, thoroughly porous "communications center" which is in "constant dialogue" with the cell it serves.

Other biologists studying bacteria, the most successful and widespread life form on our planet, now realize that we have profoundly misunderstood these seemingly simple creatures. For generations, microbes have been scrutinized in isolated captivity as laboratory specimens on petri dishes or laboratory slides. There they have been examined only as single species colonies or solitary free-rovers. This is the equivalent of studying animals in a zoo and then generalizing to the wild—which was the way chimpanzees were studied before Jane Goodall's groundbreaking observations. What one learns about a wild microbe when it is removed from its natural habitat and subjected to human control can be just as misleading.

If, on the other hand, one seeks out bacteria in their native habitat (meaning just about any place around us in the world—pipes, sewers, rocks, and pools), we perceive very different kinds of behavior. There they live "cheek by jowl," as one microbiologist phrases it, in tight, symbiotic alliances with fungi, algae, and protozoa. Together in these biofilms, microorganisms that are equipped for group living in ways never imagined become "slime cities," drawing on the same food sources and cooperating to resist threats such as antibiotics.

Finally, to bring the complexity of life closer to home, still other biologists studying "apoptosis," the cellular death that keeps our bodies whole and healthy, now speak of the life and death of cells as taking place within "cellular neighborhoods" and "communities" under "social controls." Apoptosis starts with the earliest inception of life; it appears in the embryo where it acts systematically to kill off cells by the millions in order to shape the newborn. Throughout life, cells are continually proliferating, but, thanks to apoptosis, their numbers remain constant. If a cell is infected by a virus or a harmful mutation, for safety's sake, apoptosis sets in, nudging the cell toward self-destruction. In effect, our bodies are filled with death; but because of apoptosis, dead cells are neatly scavenged and recycled by the organism. We now understand that without apoptosis, life would not be possible. In fact, when cells lose their ability to die, they run rampant, assuming that life-threatening form we call cancer. Cells have to be able to die for the good of the organism. Every cell in our body is, as one biologist puts it, "balanced on a knife edge with death on one side and growth on the other."

The process of apoptosis by which life and its development are governed is profoundly communal. The signal each cell needs to keep growing and living comes from contiguous cells. One expert in the field, Martin Raff, goes so far as to suggest that cells behave as if death were their "normal" state; suicide, he thinks, is their "default setting." Cells are kept alive as long as their "life-affirming partners" signal them to stay alive. That is why no cells, except for a cancerous one, can survive long in isolation. They need to be "encouraged" to live.

One could go on listing examples of self-organization and coordination taken from the great and small, the quick and the dead. But these few are enough to reveal a spreading perception of complexity in nature that is revising everything we know, from the structure of distant galaxies to the lowliest, most commonplace aspects of everyday life. The language we use to discuss complexity is more and more strikingly social: *collectives, cities, confederacies, partners, neighborhoods, governments, alliances.* And within these groups, we speak of things being in touch with things by way of *dialogue, signals, communication, information transfer, social controls.* Indeed, we are discovering forms of relationship so baffling that they call into question the adequacy of our most basic notions of causation, as in the case of the quantum phenomenon called "entanglement," surely nature's most subtle form of communication. Entanglement is a relationship that allows physicists to make twins of photons, and then link them in a sort of quantum web that permits instantaneous communication across light years of distance. At least thus far, entanglement stands as a relational state so strange that it eludes any causal explanation. The very antithesis of isolation and autonomy, it suggests that scientists who approach nature with a sensitivity for interaction, reciprocity, and rich interrelationship will find endless wonders.

Scientists are wisely suspicious of metaphors—at least on those rare occasions when they are conscious of using them. But they seem especially cautious about metaphors that suggest intentionality, cooperation, or altruism. If I were to suggest that the deep and pervasive organic coordination microbiologists like Lynn Margulis have observed in nature affirmed the value of friendship, care, love—soft, sentimental, "feminine" virtues—surely this would be dismissed at any scientific gathering as fuzzy-minded. But then consider the highly praised work of the popular English biologist Richard Dawkins. Dawkins is the most militant of reductionist biologists. His vision of living things remains adamantly atomistic and gleefully competitive. Identifying the genes as "the fundamental unit of selection," he pictures them struggling to survive and prevail like robber barons in the marketplace. Having isolated them out of their functioning pattern, he describes them as "selfish" and likens them to "gangsters" or "war-gamers" in order to impose a defunct Social Darwinist ethic upon their behavior.

One wishes ideas like this might be macho's last stand in the sciences. Yet as tough-minded as Dawkins may be, there are sociobiologists who have pushed the image of selfish genetic competition to even greater extremes. Some interpret the very process of reproduction as an exercise in physiological power politics, with mother and offspring waging a battle for survival in which each has to concoct strategies to outflank the other. Far from being a "harmonious collaboration," they believe "genetic conflict" lies "at the heart of gestation."

And then there is the new school of "sociobotanists," which believes the same fierce reproductive warfare can be found even among the vegetables. Thus, in an article tellingly titled "Dark Hearts: When Plants are as Murderous as Animals," we learn that "inside delicate flowers and luscious fruits lurk conflicts of interest as unforgiving as any in the animal kingdom." Exposing the "ruthless side of plants," the report winds through a discussion of "rivalry," "fratricide," "sibling murder," "greed," and "selfishness" on the part of "pugilistic pollen." Bear in mind, the authors are talking about radishes and raspberries here, not rogue elephants. The activities under study could be described as neutral pollen sorting. The macho is in the metaphors, not the phenomena.

The transition to a sense of deep community in nature is bound to be fitful precisely because it challenges the gendered values of modern science. Thus, despite the growing subtlety and complexity of modern biology, ultra-Darwinists cling to a crude ideology of masculine toughness and competition. They insist on simplifying the gene into an atom of behavioral selfishness. Where others see the elaborately orchestrated chemistry of life, they see the gene as a tiny, tough-guy particle fighting to prove his superiority and augment his inheritance. It is not hard to imagine why imagery of this kind should appeal—as it does—to entrepreneurial types and to conservative political leaders. It seems to bestow a natural mandate upon market values. But what is its appeal to biochemists, who purport to be seeking objectivity? The answer is: It preserves the gene as the biologist's version of the classical atom, an autonomous unit to whose simple, mathematical characteristics everything can be reduced. You and I, whole human beings, are, so Richard Dawkins insists, merely "survival machines, robot vehicles blindly programmed to preserve the selfish molecules known as genes." At its most fundamental level, he finds the living universe populated by John Wayne genetics and Clint Eastwood chemicals.

In a biting critique of such blatantly reductionist science, the biochemist Steven Rose observes that "The competitive, selfish genes postulated by ultra-Darwinism . . . are not genes as molecular biologists now know them." Rather, he observes, "they are a bit like atoms were before the days of nuclear physics: hard, impenetrable and indivisible billiard-balls, whose mode of interaction with one another and with their surrounding medium is limited to a collision followed by a bounce. The sole activity and telos of these genes is to create the conditions for their own replication." Such isolated, competitive units, Rose insists, could never achieve "anything like a harmoniously functioning organism." Accordingly, he offers a very different image of the gene, one in which communicative relationship and collaboration—"molecular democracy" as Rose puts it—are of the essence.

Our perception of deep community in nature was not imposed upon modern science by philosophical fiat. It has arisen gradually and internally from the scientist's admirable commitment to empirical evidence. The conscientious search into ever deeper and more distant dimensions of nature—the atoms below, the galaxies above, the hidden recesses of the organism within—has revealed an increasingly more multi-faceted picture of nature as it really is. As in an unfolding fractal image, the universe keeps opening out and out, displaying more to be studied. The more science studies the world, the more it finds. And at every level, it discovers subtle structure, rich relationships. Lewis Thomas expresses that vision with a lyricism science has for too long denied itself:

> The Earth holds together, its tissues cohere, and it has the look of a structure that really would make comprehensible sense if we only knew enough about it. From a little way off, photographed from, say, a satellite, it seems to be a kind of organism. Moreover, looked at over geologic time, it is plainly in the process of developing like an immense embryo. It is, for all its stupendous size and the numberless units and infinite variety of its life forms, coherent. Every tissue is dependent for its existence on other tissues. It is a creature, or if you want a more conventional, but less interesting term, it is a system.

"A kind of organism. . . ." In times past, the image Thomas evokes in this passage would have been called the *Anima Mundi*, the soul of the world. We can no longer envisage the

Anima Mundi as she was often drawn in medieval texts: a voluptuous, naked female with the sun on one breast, the moon on the other, and stars around her head. But for that matter, why are we so sure that philosophers as astute as Plato and Aristotle did in fact see the force that cunningly holds nature together in so naive a form? What if we simply let her be what Thomas calls her: a "system"? True, it is not the most elegant name she has been known by, but the underlying perception is the same: coherence, structure, the enhancement of life.

My colleagues in the study of history are no more prone to speculate about great transformations of consciousness than academics in other disciplines. It is likely, therefore, that two centuries hence, historians looking back upon our time may regard it as no more than a coincidence that the sciences of complexity just happened to arise during a period when women were coming into their own in so many cultural fields, bringing with them a heritage of relational sensitivities that had long been regarded as irrelevant to our understanding of nature. Historians then may not see any greater connection between the one and the other than most now see between patriarchal values and atomistic science. On the other hand, in that distant era, we may have become so sensitized to the subtle relationships that bind reality together that all scholars will recognize that our appreciation of the infinite relatedness of things had much to do with the demise of gender bias.

10
The Black Madonna

I thought I had found all I needed to take home from Switzerland in Geneva. But Betty had one more item on her itinerary. She wanted to visit the abbey at Einsiedeln in the Catholic, German-speaking region of Switzerland. I did not know it until we reached the town, but for someone who had set himself the task of writing a feminist *Frankenstein*, this would be as important a part of the trip as the Villa Diodati or Chamonix.

Einsiedeln is the birthplace of one of the most remarkable characters in Western history. Born in 1493 as Theophrastus Bombastus von Hohenheim, he is better remembered by the name Paracelsus. Here and there about the town plaques and booklets remind the visitor that Paracelsus was the founding father of modern medicine. He is the man who hit upon the simple but revolutionary idea that diseases ought to be carefully studied one by one and then treated with specific remedies, rather than attributed to vague supernatural humors. As advanced as he was in some respects, Paracelsus still clung to tradition. Many of his medicines were borrowed from the folk healers and witches of his day whose skill with herbs he greatly admired. He was also an alchemist of great repute who claimed to have found the secret of creating life in a test tube. That is why Mary placed him at the top of young Victor Frankenstein's reading list. The being Paracelsus supposedly coaxed into existence was a transparent little man, a homunculus, who originated from semen kept hermetically sealed in a glass retort at the temperature of a mare's womb. Fed on human blood for forty weeks, the homunculus might grow into a full-sized man capable of reason. Paracelsus might have been worth a novel in his own right.

But Betty and I did not go to Einsiedeln in search of Frankensteinian alchemy. We were there to see the Black Madonna.

What seemed at first a mere side trip would finish by teaching me how historically deep the sexual politics of modern science reach—perhaps all the way back to the Paleolithic era, long before men began to have fantasies, whether alchemical or biochemical, of producing their own unmothered progeny.

THE CHURCH THAT stands at the heart of Einsiedeln has been twice rebuilt over the centuries. In its latest, eighteenth-century incarnation, it is an architectural confection that presses Baroque to its flamboyant extreme. Trumpet-blowing angels in swirling gowns, their gleaming wings outspread, stand poised to leap from the cornices; pink stucco cherubs frolic beneath the soaring vaults; gilded roses twine around the columns. The white plaster trim that drips over the salmon-colored marble walls might be frosting on a wedding cake.

The train ride from Geneva to Einsiedeln takes only a few hours, but culturally speaking it is a journey from one world to another. The contrast between the two towns recalls a wrenching transition in Western spiritual life. Standing amid the riotous decor of Einsiedeln Abbey, I thought back to Geneva, where the city's cathedral still stands as zealous Calvinist reformers left it four centuries ago, stripped of every vestige of "popish" art and ornamentation. Nothing remains but the bleak bare walls and the pulpit. It is as if, by some law of aesthetic compensation, the adornment that had been so sternly repressed in Geneva somehow made its way across Switzerland to resurface all the more boisterously at Einsiedeln.

A thousand years before the town was graced with its Rococo church, Einsiedeln was a place of pilgrimage. And like all pilgrimage sites, Einsiedeln has its lore. In the year 861, so the legend goes, St. Meinrad the Hermit, who had retired to the Dark Forest to live a life of prayer, was murdered by thieves. Two ravens followed his killers and betrayed them to the law. His followers were inspired to consecrate a monastery where his blood had been spilled. But long before St. Meinrad arrived, there was a shrine to the Blessed Virgin in this place. It is still there, now engulfed by the abbey and the surrounding marketplace where scores of vendors hawk religious trinkets and souvenirs.

In its vestibule, the church shelters an altar on which a quaintly doll-like wooden figure stands in a gilded aureole with bowers of fresh roses at her feet. This is the gravitational center of Einsiedeln. By the busload each day, people come seeking grace and healing. The scene can sometimes resemble a Fellini movie, thronging and garish. People in wheelchairs wait at the portal saying their rosaries. Children bearing bouquets and banners march up to the altar singing. At the appointed hour, the monks come to chant the *Salve Regina* outside the Lady Chapel. After each ceremony, the figure is ceremoniously re-costumed in a brocaded and jewelled gown of a different color, a practice that makes her seem like a celestial Barbie doll. She is what people come to see, because Einsiedeln's Virgin is special. She is a Black Madonna, one of the few in Christendom.

Over the centuries, the original figure was supposedly blackened by smoke from votive candles, so the latest version was carved from ebony. But those who have studied the Black Madonnas of Europe have another interpretation. Black is the color of Earth, the sign of the ancient Mother Goddess. "Black Madonnas," one scholar observes, "may be considered a metaphor for a memory of the time when the Earth was believed to be the body of a woman and all creatures were equal, a memory transmitted in vernacular traditions of Earth-bonded cultures. What all Black Madonnas have in common is location on or near archaeological evidence of the pre-Christian woman divinity. . . ." At Einsiedeln, as at so many places in the Christian world, the old religion was assimilated to the new with only a thin veneer of orthodoxy covering the indigenous cultural history that lies beneath. That connection is made even clearer on the steps outside the church. There a bronze Virgin welcomes visitors from atop a fountain. This figure of the Madonna, holding her divine child, is crowned by stars and stands atop a crescent moon, unmistakable emblems of the nature goddess from whom the Virgin has inherited her place.

If Jean Calvin, the father of Puritanism, had ever come to Einsiedeln, he would have excoriated all he saw as pagan idolatry. In one sense, he would have been right. There is no mistaking the Black Madonna for anything but a surrogate fertility goddess. That is what the Virgin became wherever Christianity moved into heathen territory, the convenient bridge between cultures. She even crossed the sea to the New World traveling with Christian missionaries to become the Virgin of Guadalupe.

Calvin, an exacting prophet of the Father God, could never have understood why that dark, earthy image has proven to be so persistent. He never realized how deep her roots penetrate into human culture. The Black Madonna vastly predates his struggle with Catholic Mariolatry—the adoration of the Virgin. One might even say that, in a curious way, she has returned to find a place in our own scientific society.

In 1536, when the young Calvin was invited to become the spiritual city manager of Geneva, his charge was to create a perfect Christian community. He began his regime by unleashing an iconoclast fury upon the city. Calvin was determined to drive out every last trace of the Whore of Babylon, as he called the Church of Rome. For Calvin, reform began with a great stripping-down operation. Calvin's Christianity was fiercely literal, a religion that permitted no imagery, no decoration, no complexity, nothing on which the eye might loiter while the mind was concentrated on Scripture, the Word that was the only road to God. Under his stern guidance, Geneva became the fortress of Puritanism, that dour version of Protestantism that regarded all imagery as idolatry and all merriment as the devil's work. Some historians believe it is unfair to exaggerate the austerity of Calvinism. Perhaps no religion was ever entirely joyless and life-denying. But Calvin's faith surely comes closest. His famous *Institutes* are legalistically austere to the point of deadly rigidity.

Scientists might not see any connection between Calvin's rigorously dogmatic theology and science as they know it, but that is a matter of historical ignorance on their part. Without realizing it, they owe more to Calvin than they do to Galileo— or perhaps a better way to put it would be: If it were not for Calvin's influence in Protestant countries, Galileo's science would have had no future in any part of Europe. That is because if it were not for the Puritanical intolerance of symbolism, ritual, and iconography, early modern thought might have remained as congested with religious and metaphysical imagery as in medieval times.

Calvin's Reformation, especially as it was filtered through the mind of the Puritan genius Francis Bacon, gave the new philosophy of science what it most needed: a clean slate, a *tabula rasa*. Once Calvin was finished, only the distant lawgiver God remained as an appropriate object of worship, a stern, patriarchal deity that was out of and above nature. No saints, no angels, no intercessors or intermediaries. Above all, no Virgin Mother. She who had occupied so central a place in the old religion was the major casualty of Protestantism.

The cult of Mary, on which so much ritual, art, prayer, and theology had once been lavished, was abruptly ended in Protestant countries. For Calvin, anything that came between God and His believers—even a mental picture—was an idol. Some Calvinist divines identified an "idol" as anything "feigned in the mind by imagination." There is a haunting similarity between such teachings and Galileo's bold attack upon what he called "secondary qualities" in nature. Galileo, seeking to pare the world down to its abstract mathematical essence, concluded that everything the senses registered was but superficial appearance, a lesser realm. Only quantities were *really* real. These days, when theoretical physicists censor the public's spontaneous visualizing response by warning us we must not try to picture the underlying nature of the world, whether atoms or quarks or preons, they are drawing upon an intellectual discipline devised by Calvin. Reality is beyond the senses; only the rigorously logical mind, leaping bravely into the intangible, can grasp it. *No images.*

But a cosmos composed of wandering particles in the void is a cold place to make one's home. The science that has envisioned such a world is as severe as Calvin's theology, which sought to justify the ways of a God who could, for His own sovereign and inscrutable purposes, predestine a newborn baby to burn in Hell. Along that course, science opens the way into Jacques Monod's "frozen universe of solitude," a vision of the world that has "nothing to recommend it but a certain Puritan arrogance."

In times past, when a troubled humanity sought consolation in life, it looked to a warmer presence who was always a mother: Isis, Cybele, Kuan Yin, Magna Mater, the Blessed Virgin. How often has human culture oscillated between these poles of rigor and mercy, the tough mind, the soft heart? Now it seems our own scientific culture has begun to swing away from the severe atomistic logic that denied nature its nurturing warmth. In no literal sense can we expect the Black Madonna to return. We have passed beyond goddesses that wear a human form. Our universe will continue to be a place of quarks and galaxies, genes and molecules. But the rigor of the old cosmology, the eternal void where chance reigned and the cry of the heart went unanswered, is yielding to the perception that all physical entities are bound together in deep community, that the universe itself, for all its immensity, seems unaccountably destined by its initial conditions to become the womb of life and mind.

Admittedly, any sentence that contains the word "destined" steps beyond the realm of science. But then a surprising number of scientists, honestly impressed by the artful complexity of the world, can now be found taking just that step. Exploring the paradoxical implications of physics at the quantum level, John Wheeler has suggested that "observers may be necessary to bring the universe into being." Other scientists, pondering the wealth of coincidences that have come together in concert to make the phenomenon of life possible, wonder if there is some hidden necessity at work that has mandated the appearance of life and mind. Called the anthropic principle, the main significance to this highly tentative line of conjecture is simply that it exists at all as a serious talking point among scientists. For example, the mathematical physicist Paul Davies, wondering if life and consciousness have a special place in the universe, admits that "the natural world is not just any old concoction of entities and forces, but a marvelously ingenious and unified mathematical system." Does that ingenuity betoken destiny? His inclination is to answer yes, it has "a genuine transcendent reality."

Those who seek comfort amid the tribulations of life or a sense of greater purpose are still better off turning to the Black Madonna than to physics, where ideas like the anthropic principle are apt to remain a slender, speculative reed to lean one's heart against. But the scientists are beginning to grant small mercies that nobody could have predicted when atoms ruled the universe.

II

"only connect!"

Frankenstein was published anonymously. Mary's publisher claimed the book was too shocking to bear a woman's name. But there may have been another motive. Lackington, the only publishing house that would take the book, regarded Mary as an amateur, and apparently a not very talented one. The firm seemed determined to do all it could to associate Percy, the better known name, with the book. Lackington may even have started the rumor, after Mary's authorship was revealed, that Percy's revisions of the story were so extensive that he ought to be named as her collaborator. Scholars now see this as an untenable exaggeration. Lackington's real intent may have been to eclipse the unknown wife in favor of the famous husband. Percy tried to help with Mary's fledgling literary career; he even went so far as to place a preface on the book vouching for its credibility. Speaking for his wife, he assured readers that "the event on which this fiction is founded has been supposed . . . as not of impossible occurrence."

Mary accepted her husband's dubious favors in the same deferential spirit in which she had accepted the corrections he added where the text dealt with science. From the moment the story first entered her mind, she had not presumed to speak with any authority on matters of natural philosophy. In Geneva, where she had sat through the late-night conversations in which Percy and Byron discussed "the nature of the principle of life," she described herself as "a devout but nearly silent listener." Great men were talking— and about science. Mary's diary shows that she was reading as much science as Percy was during these years—Baron Holberg, Buffon, Fontonelle, Voltaire, Robert Bage. Even so, she had to remain silent. Science was not meant for ladies, nor would it be for nearly the next hundred years. At the century's end, Marie Curie, whose research would help prove the atom was not atomistic, had to learn all the physics she knew from her father. No schools were open to her.

Now all this has changed. Or has it? Women have won the chance to prove themselves in every field of science— meaning, they have shown that anything a man can learn, do, and achieve, a woman can learn, do, and achieve as well. But *gender* as distinct from individual accomplishment remains a sticking point. Women enter the sciences; but "womanliness"—those qualities that have always been stereotypically attributed to females—is not yet entirely welcome, whether it comes into the laboratory wearing pants or a skirt.

Are the sexes really races, each with its own code of morality, and their mutual love a mere device of Nature's to keep things going? . . . Her judgement told her no. She knew that out of Nature's device we have built a magic that will win us immortality. Far more mysterious than the call of sex to sex is the tenderness that we throw into that call; far wider is the gulf between us and the farmyard and the garbage that nourishes it. We are evolving, in ways that Science cannot measure, to ends that Theology dares not contemplate.

E. M. Forster, Howard's End

THE CASE FOR admitting women to the study of science is a matter of simple political justice. It is the same case Mary Wollstonecraft long ago made for the rights of woman: judge women by their aptitude, not by their reproductive organs. But feminist psychology has drawn our attention to another, more far-reaching aspect of sexism in the scientific community. Because girls are raised to specialize in a certain set of human characteristics, would they not, then, bring to science a different sensibility? Does that sensibility have a right to be represented in science — or, for that matter, in business, politics, law, or medicine?

Here, I want to be careful how I phrase this important distinction. There is no question that stereotypes impose an injustice on the individuals they encumber. Stereotypes prejudge and distort the personality. But not all stereotypes embody negative qualities. In the case of stereotypic femininity, we are dealing with many qualities that some would say were of the highest cultural value: tenderness, receptivity, sympathy, gentleness, the self-in-relation. Londa Schiebinger makes the point that

"who does science affects the kind of science that gets done."
No doubt. But what will the result be if, upon entering science,
women deliberately leave behind the qualities of mind and
heart that stem from the self-in-relation? They have proven they
can do so. In politics and business, women have shown that
they can be "one of the boys." Surely they can pursue macho
science as well as any man. But are we then saying that *only* the
stereotypic masculine qualities belong in the profession? If that
is the price we exact for integrating women into science, then
doing justice to the individual may impoverish the culture.

When Jane Goodall submitted her first professional paper to
the *Annals of the New York Academy of Science*, the journal
requested certain changes. It wanted her to drop the names she
had given the chimps she had studied and use numbers
instead. The journal also corrected her use of "he" and "she"
for the animals she would one day call "my friends." The journal wanted them referred to as "it." Goodall refused. The most
important part of her research lay in the relationship she had
built up with the chimps.

In her study of Jane Goodall, Dian Fossey, and Biruté
Galdikas, Sy Montgomery comments on how women have rev-
olutionized the science of ethology:

> In the masculine world of Western science, where achieve-
> ment is typically measured by mastery, theirs was an unusual
> approach. It was no accident that Louis Leakey, the paleo-
> anthropologist who launched these long-term studies of the
> great apes, chose three women to lead the research.
> Although certain men have also learned how to relinquish
> control, the approach seems particularly feminine. The
> approach allows choice and the nurturing of a relationship
> on the Other's terms.

Jane Goodall's approach, as Montgomery observes, emphasized "relationships rather than rules . . . receptivity rather than control. . . . She was applying a feminine approach to a field that was dominated and defined by male views and values. . . . Jane's strength is that she relinquished control." That was what Louis Leakey wanted when he brought the now-famous trio of "ape women" into his circle. He believed they would make better observers.

But why? Because they were more patient. And why were they more patient? Presumably because they were in no hurry to prove themselves, publish, build a career, and get ahead. They were willing to take years to follow and observe, to enter respectfully into the life of the apes, especially to attend to personality and to the details of mother-child relations. Leakey was, in effect, recruiting for a special set of talents he felt he could find more readily among women. He wanted a passivity—an *alert* passivity—that was practically unprecedented in Western science. The only near approach to such watchful passivity might be found in astronomy, where the objects are hopelessly beyond manipulation. Even so, astronomers have found ways to act upon light, to fracture it and analyze it into its rudimentary properties. Admittedly, that has taught us a great deal. But the German Romantic poet Goethe, who made his own strange study of light from an artistic perspective, questioned even that much interference with nature. He wondered at what point our instruments might be creating what we think we see out there in the world. Though his reservations may have been extreme, his question is still a good one. Every science of active observation must take care not to get lost among its own artifacts.

Goodall and her colleagues, who now include many male ethologists, have shown us what Montgomery calls "the glimmerings of a new way of doing science." At the very least, their methods show up well in the wildlife television documentaries that are now teaching people more science than they are learning in classrooms. All of us have seen the now-famous photo that shows the hand of a chimp reaching out to touch Goodall's forehead. That image deserves to be an emblem of our time fully as much as that of the Earth photographed from space. But, as Donna Haraway asks, "What is the history of this touch? . . . From whose point of view is distance calibrated and closeness negotiated?" If, as Haraway suggests, that touch is "redemptive," we should remember that the human being in the picture is a woman who came to the wilds in friendship, with no need to conquer, no intention of capturing and carrying off.

Quite as remarkable as the achievement of Jane Goodall and her colleagues is the public acclaim their work has gained against all the odds. People understand this work and respond to it warmly. Relating to the great apes as "friends," giving them names, and studying them as personalities in their true habitat (or as close to that as the ever-encroaching modern world permits) has come to have a persuasive public appeal. I suspect the gentleness of this method calls out to us. We see in it a new way of connecting with nature that seems peculiarly appropriate to our times. Why should that be? Is it perhaps our growing appreciation of the relational self that has helped cleanse "the doors of perception"? If so, that may be a greater contribution than any set of findings Goodall has offered.

Evelyn Fox Keller has used the work of Nobel Prize-winning biologist Barbara McClintock as a model for giving scientific status to this new sensibility, "a feeling for the organism," as she calls it. McClintock, who discovered the "jumping gene," developed the habit of treating everything she studied as if it had an "autobiography." In one difficult exercise in cytological analysis, she employed what she called "a form of attention" that made her "part of the system" of chromosomes she was studying. "I was right down there with them," she reports, "and everything got big. I was even able to see the internal parts of the chromosomes—actually everything was there. It surprised me because I actually felt as if I was right down there and these were my friends." Keller believes such an empathic sensibility can permeate the scientific community as a whole. We must, she comments, "reconstruct our understanding of science in terms born out of the diverse spectrum of human experience rather than out of the narrow spectrum that our culture has labeled masculine."

"Biology," as the biochemist Mae-Wan How dramatically observes, "has a long tradition of fixing, pinning, clamping, pressing, pulping, homogenizing, extracting and fractionating; all of which has given rise to, and reinforced, a static and atomistic view of the organism." Like Barbara McClintock, she favors "allowing the system to inform." As she puts it, "we must find ways of *communicating* with the system itself, rather than interrogating it, or worse, testing it to destruction. This is the reason why sensitive, noninvasive techniques of investigation are essential for really getting to know the living system."

These formal epistemological issues are anticipated in *Frankenstein* by a single, striking literary device. Mary gives Victor Frankenstein *a specimen that talks back.* That, after all, is what the monster is: nature at large speaking up to the scientist. The monster, knowing he is nothing in Victor's eyes but the remnant of a botched experiment, challenges his maker: "You, my creator, would tear me to pieces and triumph; remember that, and tell me why I should pity man more than he pities me? You would not call it murder if you could precipitate me into one of those ice-drifts and destroy my frame, the work of your own hands." The words with which the "thing he had created" ends his indictment of the first mad scientist might be the voice of all the wounded Earth crying out to its dominant species. "Mine shall not be the submission of abject slavery. I will revenge my injuries. If I cannot inspire love, I will cause fear. . . . Have a care; I will work at your destruction, nor finish until I desolate your heart, so that you shall curse the hour of your birth."

Exactly how the relational self may one day reach out to the quarks and quasars is not yet clear. But then we should remember how long it has taken modern science to create the method that it has for so long believed will guarantee total objectivity. Great transformations of consciousness do not happen overnight. The relational self will not be able to address everything in nature in the same face-to-face, hand-in-hand way in which humans and other animals can relate. But the bond of sympathy, like the artist's eye for beauty, may stretch across many divisions. Healing our alienation from the more than human world may start quite close at hand. My thesis in this essay has focused on the way in which the gender stereotypes that govern the homes, schools, playgrounds, and workplaces where boys become men and girls become women have cut us off from the full powers of the relational self. How do we refashion our relationship to the universe at large? Perhaps by attending to the subtle sexual politics of everyday life.

E. M. Forster's novel *Howard's End* ranks among the most searching studies of gender in modern literature. The story does not deal with science, but it does concern the heavy price we pay for gender bias in our lives as a whole. The single moral commandment of the novel is delivered by his female protagonist, but the words are those of a male author, and so demonstrate that all of us can, at least to some degree, rise above the assigned identities we are born into:

> Only connect! That was the whole of her sermon. Only
> connect the prose and the passion, and both will be exalted,
> and human love will be seen at its highest. Live in frag-
> ments no longer. Only connect, and the beast and the
> monk, robbed of the isolation that is life to either, will die.

Once we were told on the highest authority that the universe was no more than atoms adrift in the void; now we are learning that we live amid "patterns that interlock to infinity," as one of the displays at CERN puts it. Our growing sense of the depth, complexity, and organic subtlety of nature on both the microcosmic and the macrocosmic scale is not a minor change of view; it is radical enough to be ethically wrenching. We are discovering that natural philosophy needs bonds of sympathy as well as precision of intellect. But above all, this great change is delightfully surprising. None of the founding fathers of science could have imagined that one day Dame Nature would prove to be so charmingly clever.

Perhaps that is what John Wheeler, among the leading quantum theorists, means when he predicts that "there may be no such thing as the 'glittering central mechanism of the universe' to be seen behind a glass wall at the end of the trail. Not machinery but magic may be the better description of the treasure that is waiting."

AFTERWORD

THE IDOLS OF THE BEDCHAMBER

THIS BOOK BEGAN in a bedchamber, in the room where Victor Frankenstein realized that his bride Elizabeth had been taken from him by the monster he created. Storytellers have always valued the bedroom as a setting for literature. It is a place of birth and death. It is also where men and women come together in the full power of their sexual identities. That makes it a place for highly charged drama. But perhaps it can also provide an occasion for philosophical reflection. At least that is how I have been using Elizabeth's fatal bedchamber in these pages.

Four centuries ago Francis Bacon, foremost among the founding father of modern science, warned that "the human understanding is like a false mirror, which, receiving rays irregularly, distorts and discolors the nature of things by mingling its own nature with it." Bacon's rhetoric has an antique ring to it, but what he was addressing is, in fact, a matter of enduring importance. He had succeeded in framing the most important question any scientist can ask: *Am I seeing things as they really are?*

Bacon cautioned that, as objective as scientists try to be, they may still be led astray by "false notions" whose influence they cannot detect. "The human understanding," he wisely recognized, "is no dry light, but receives an infusion from the will and affections." He used a religious figure of speech to characterize these mischievous notions; he called them "idols," as if they were false gods that distracted us from the truth. There were, he believed, four such idols. He called them the idols of the tribe, the cave, the marketplace, and the theater. The names are quaint, but each continues to merit critical attention as a form of intellectual contamination. Together, they make it impossible for us to take the "measure of the universe."

Here, at the birth of modern science, is a fundamental insight. Our knowledge of nature Out There begins with knowledge of ourselves In Here. Until we have freed our minds and emotions of the hidden presuppositions that stand between us and the world, we can never be certain we are in touch with reality.

As precocious as Bacon was in raising this great dilemma, he failed to recognize one distortion that has warped our vision of nature ever since his day. He never included among his idols the gender bias that he and his colleagues were reading into the world around them by the very fact that they regarded nature as "she."

Had he been more sensitive to his own limitations, Bacon might have added one more mental quirk to his list of idols: the idols of the bedchamber, the preconceptions about sexual identity that every scientist inherits in childhood. The myths of gender work at so deep a level in us that it would take more than extraordinary personal awareness to bring them into the light of day. That took a social movement. For a frank discussion of the emotional forces behind man-woman relations, we have had to wait until a distinctly feminist psychology emerged in our own time. Will the sciences, still among the most gender-biased institutions in our society, be courageous enough to restore "the woman in us" to her rightful place? That will take a frankness even greater than the great paradigm shifts that mark the history of scientific thought.

Once, in the dim reaches of prehistory, our ancestors experienced nature as a Great Mother. In later times, the natural world came more and more to be imprinted with images of the power-seeking male ego. Beyond both of these lies a gender-free science that can be pursued by men and women who have chosen their own identity in the laboratory, in the field, and in daily life. Though we may never see the world around us with a wholly unbiased eye, we can with each new era seek to transcend the distortions that plagued the last. At least with respect to gender, we may be close to a vision of nature unburdened by the sexual politics that have warped our personal lives and our environmental relations.

And what wonders will that universe reveal!

Notes

Page 12:   **the search for a fundamental datum in psychology:**
Abraham Maslow, *The Psychology of Science* (New York:
Harper & Row, 1966), p. 3.

Page 13:   **act like men:** Margaret Eisenhart and Elizabeth Finkel,
*Women's Science: Learning and Succeeding from the
Margins* (Chicago: University of Chicago Press, 1998.)

Page 14:   **As Londa Schiebinger has argued:** Londa Schiebinger,
Nature's Body: Gender in the Making of Modern Science
(Boston: Beacon Press, 1993), p. 3.

Page 34:   **Blam! Blam! Blam! Blam!:** Robert J. Coontz Jr., "Out of
Thin Air," *The Sciences*, July/August 1996, p. 11.

Page 41:   **have dismissed it to the realms of metaphysics:** Quoted
in Edward MacKinnon, *Scientific Explanation and
Atomic Physics* (Chicago: University of Chicago Press,
1982), p. 101. MacKinnon's book is a magisterial study of
the controversies surrounding the atomic paradigm at the
turn of the twentieth century.

Page 42:   **the French physicist Pierre Curie:** Brian Easlea incisively reviews the strange partnership between Pierre and Marie Curie from the viewpoint of sexual politics in *Fathering the Unthinkable: Masculinity. Scientists, and the Nuclear Arms Race* (London: Pluto Press, 1983), pp. 44–48.

Page 43:   **It is fear of the labyrinthine flux and complexity:** Aldous Huxley, from his essay "Wordsworth in the Tropics," *Collected Essays* (New York: Bantam Books, 1966).

Page 44:   **Stephen H. Kellert observes:** Stephen H. Kellert, *In the Wake of Chaos: Unpredictable Order in Dynamical Systems* (Chicago: University of Chicago Press, 1993), p. 155.

Page 51:   **out of the fusion of relativity:** Steven Weinberg, *Dreams of a Final Theory* (New York: Pantheon Books, 1995), p. 25.

Page 52:   **concentrations and knots in a fundamental, continuous field:** David Bohm and F. David Peat, *Science, Order, and Creativity* (New York: Bantam Books, 1987).

Page 54:   **"tickling" and "nudging":** Timothy Paul Smith, "Worlds Within Worlds," *The Sciences*, July/August, 1996, p. 29.

Page 56:   **the feminist theologian and psychologist Catherine Keller:** Catherine Keller's *From a Broken Web: Separation, Sexism, and Self* (Boston: Beacon Press, 1986) is one of the best surveys of feminist psychology, with special reference to issues in science. See especially pp. 240–248 for her psychological analysis of time and space in modern physics.

Page 57: **the archetypal female, Mother Nature:** N. Katherine Hayles, *The Cosmic Web: Scientific Field Models and Literary Strategies in the Twentieth Century* (Ithaca, NY: Cornell University Press, 1984), pp. 87–8. See also Evelyn Fox Keller, "Cognitive Repression in Contemporary Physics," *American Journal of Physics* 47 (August 1979), pp. 718–21.

Page 59: **the Skinner Box:** The Skinner Box is presented in B. F. Skinner's novel *Walden Two* (New York: Macmillan Company, 1948) as the basis for a fully scientific Utopian community.

Page 59: **But in the judgment of child psychologist Jean Liedloff:** Jean Liedloff, *The Continuum Concept* (New York: Alfred A. Knopf, 1977).

Page 72: **As the feminist cultural critic Charlene Spretnak sees it:** Charlene Spretnak, *States of Grace: The Recovery of Meaning in the Postmodern Age* (New York: Harper Collins, 1991), pp. 245–246.

Page 72: **the monster, the enemy, and the Amazon:** Catherine Keller, *From a Broken Web: Separation, Sexism, and Self* (Boston: Beacon Press, 1986), p. 26. The feminist reinterpretation of prehistory draws heavily on the archaeological research of Marija Gimbutas. See Gimbutas, *Goddesses and Gods of Old Europe* (Los Angeles: University of California Press, 1982) and *The Civilization of the Goddess* (San Francisco: HarperCollins, 1991).

Page 72: **By masculinist epistemology:** Ellyn Kaschak, *Engendered Lives* (New York: Basic Books, 1992), p. 11.

Page 73: **alternative life-histories of the same metaphor:** Christopher Small, *Ariel Like a Harpy: Shelley, Mary, and Frankenstein* (London: Gollancz, 1972), p. 240.

Page 77: **The first operation I ever saw:** Abraham Maslow, *The Psychology of Science* (New York: Harper & Row, 1966), p. 139.

Page 82: **It is hard to realize:** Steven Weinberg, *The First Three Minutes: A Modern View of the Origin of the Universe* (New York: Basic Books, 1977), p. 154.

Page 83: **the world's uncaring emptiness:** Jacques Monod, *Chance and Necessity* (New York: A. A. Knopf, 1971), p. 180.

Page 83: **Cosmic Cannibals:** Ken Croswell, "Cosmic Cannibals," *New Scientist*, July 12, 1997, pp. 31–32.

Page 83: **One hypothesis formulated by Lee Smolin:** Lee Smolin, *The Life of the Cosmos* (New York: Oxford University Press, 1997).

Page 85: **a crucial differentiating experience:** Nancy Chodorow, *Feminism and Psychoanalytic Theory* (New Haven, CT: Yale University Press, 1989), pp. 45–46.

Page 86: **Catherine Keller adds:** Catherine Keller, *From a Broken Web* (Boston: Beacon Press, 1986), p. 126.

Page 88: **The self-identity of the boy child:** Marti Kheel, "Ecofeminism and Deep Ecology," in *Reweaving the World: The Emergence of Ecofeminism*, ed. Irene Diamond, et al. (San Francisco: Sierra Club Books, 1990), p. 129. For the most influential feminist extension of Object Relations theory, see Nancy Chodorow, *The Reproduction of*

Mothering: Psychoanalysis and the Sociology of Gender (Los Angeles: University of California Press, 1978), and *Feminism and Psychoanalytic Theory* (New Haven, CT: Yale University Press, 1989).

Page 88: **It would seem that the sense of self inflicted upon males:** Catherine Keller, "Toward a Postpatriarchal Postmodernity," in *Spirituality and Society*, ed. David Ray Griffin (Albany, NY: State University of New York Press, 1988), p.72.

Page 88: **Our early maternal environment:** Evelyn Fox Keller, "Feminism and Science," *Signs: Journal of Women and Society* (Spring 1982): p. 595.

Page 89: **As Dan Kindlon and Michael Thompson observe:** Dan Kindlon and Michael Thompson, *Raising Cain: Protecting the Emotional Life of Boys* (New York: Balantine Books, 1999), p. 79.

Page 89: **"The ideal self," Ellyn Kaschak observes:** Ellyn Kaschak, *Engendered Lives* (New York: Basic Books, 1992), p. 149.

Page 89: **Carol Gilligan puts the same point more colorfully:** Carol Gilligan, *In A Different Voice: Psychological Theory and Women's Development* (Cambridge, MA: Harvard University Press, 1982), p. 28.

Page 91: **regressive moods of omnipotence and insecurity:** Paul Shepard, *Nature and Madness* (San Francisco: Sierra Club Books, 1982), p. 126.

Page 100: **The veneration wherewith men are imbued:** Robert Boyle, *The Works* (London: Reprografischer Nachdruck der Ausg., 1772), IV, 363.

Page 100: **whether of health, or riches, or sensual delight:** Robert Boyle, *The Works* (London: Reprografischer Nachdruck der Ausg., 1772), I, 310.

Page 104: **For the idea of a morphological cell:** Franz Leydig, quoted in Stephen Toulmin and June Goodfield, *The Architecture of Matter* (New York: Harper & Row, 1962), pp. 352, 355.

Page 104: **Alfred North Whitehead, writing in 1925:** Alfred North Whitehead, *Science and the Modern World* (New York: Mentor Books, 1925), p. 97.

Page 105: **Rape, as Susan Brownmiller reminds us:** Susan Brownmiller, *Against Our Will: Men, Women and Rape* (New York: Simon & Schuster, 1975), p. 15. As definitive as Brownmiller's study is, it says nothing about rape as it relates to the natural environment.

Page 105: **a "pseudosexual act":** A. Nicholas Groth, *Men Who Rape: The Psychology of the Offender* (New York: Plenum Press, 1979), p. 25.

Page 112: **the *soror mystica* or mystic sister:** Mircea Eliade, *The Forge and the Crucible: The Origins and Structures of Alchemy* (New York: Harper Torchbooks, 1962) and Allison Coudert, *Alchemy: The Philosopher's Stone* (Boulder, CO: Shambhala Books, 1980) cover the erotic aspects of alchemy. Johannes Fabricus' *Alchemy: The Medieval Alchemists and their Royal Art* (London: Diamond Books, 1976) gives attention to the shadowy figure of the mystic sister.

Page 124: **the theoretical biologist Stuart Kauffman:** Stuart Kauffman, *At Home in the Universe: The Search for Laws of Self-Organization and Complexity* (New York: Oxford University Press, 1995), pp. 303–304.

Page 125: **we belong to this universe:** Hubert Reeves, in "The Unexpected Universe," part three of *The Space Age*, PBS series, broadcast November 1992. Also see Reeves' most recent work, *The Hour of Our Delight* (New York: Freeman, 1993).

Page 125: **The philosopher of science, Henry Stapp:** Henry Stapp, "Quantum Theory and the Physicist's Conception of Nature," in *The World View of Contemporary Physics*, ed. Richard Kitchener (State University of New York Press, 1988), p. 54.

Page 126: **a new kind of cellular government:** Lynn Margulis and Dorian Sagan, *Microcosmos: Four Billion Years of Microbial Evolution* (New York: Summit Books, 1986), pp. 117–119.

Page 127: **cooperating to resist threats such as antibiotics:** Andy Coghlan, "Slime City," *New Scientist*, August 31, 1996, pp. 32–5.

Page 128: **balanced on a knife edge:** Kate Douglas, "Making Friends with Death-Wish Genes," *New Scientist*, July 30, 1994, pp. 31–33. Also see Martin Raff, "Death Wish," *The Sciences*, July/August 1996, pp. 94–7.

Page 130: **mother and offspring waging a battle for survival:** David Haig, "Altercation of Generations: Genetic

Conflicts of Pregnancy," *American Journal of Repro-ductive Immunology*, March 1996, 226–232.

Page 130: **the new school of "sociobotanists":** Bryant Furlow, "Flower Power," *New Scientist*, January 9, 1999, pp. 23–26. It should be noted that much of the research in sociobotany has been carried out by women, a telling indication that the masculine gender bias that shows up in these metaphors is grounded in the profession more than in the person.

Page 131: **the biochemist Steven Rose observes:** Steven Rose, *Lifelines: Biology Beyond Determinism* (New York: Oxford University Press, 1998), p. 210.

Page 132: **The Earth holds together:** Lewis Thomas, "Notes of a Biology-Watcher, *The New England Journal of Medicine* (June 29, 1978), 298(26): 1454–6.

Page 138: **Black Madonnas . . . may be considered a metaphor:** Lucia Birnbaum, *Black Madonnas* (Boston: Northeastern University Press, 1993), p. 3.

Page 142: **the mathematical physicist Paul Davies:** Paul Davies, *The Mind of God* (New York: Simon and Schuster, 1992), pp. 213–214.

Page 146: **In the masculine world of Western science:** Sy Montgomery, *Walking with the Great Apes* (Boston: Houghton-Mifflin, 1991), pp. xvi, 102.

Page 148: **Evelyn Fox Keller has used the work:** Evelyn Fox Keller, *Reflections on Gender and Science* (New Haven, CT: Yale University Press, 1985), p. 176.

Page 149: **and these were my friends:** Barbara McClintock, quoted in Evelyn Fox Keller, *Reflections on Gender and Science* (New Haven, CT: Yale University Press, 1985), p. 165. Also see Keller, *A Feeling for the Organism: The Life and Work of Barbara McClintock* (New York: Freeman, 1983).

Page 149: **as the biochemist Mae-Wan Ho dramatically observes:** Mae-Wan Ho, *The Rainbow and the Worm* (London and Singapore: World Scientific Press, 1993), pp. 111, 167–168.

Page 151: **Not machinery but magic may be the better description:** John Wheeler, quoted in Nick Herbert, *Quantum Reality: Beyond the New Physics* (New York: Anchor Books, 1985), p. 29.

Page 154: **he called them "idols":** Bacon's famous passage on the idols can be found among the Aphorisms in Book 1 of *The New Organon*.

Bibliography

The Gendered Atom draws upon a sizeable body of writing in the field of feminist psychology. The field, and the movement connected with it, have been growing since the mid-1970s. Taken as a whole, feminist psychology represents a courageous revision of all mainstream psychological and therapeutic schools. By way of a critique of gender roles, feminist psychologists are redefining every category in psychology. They have shown that key concepts like sanity, normality, development, ego-strength, rationality, maturity, adulthood, consciousness, and the unconscious have all been gender-biased toward a patriarchal male model of the self.

The principle early studies in the field include Phyllis Chesler, *Women and Madness* (London: Allen Lane, 1974) and the work of Jean Baker Miller, especially *Psychoanalysis and Women: Contributions to a New Theory and Therapy* (New York: Brunner/Mazel, 1973) and *Toward a New Psychology of Women* (Boston: Beacon Press, 1976). As director of the Stone Center at Wellesley College, Miller has played a central role in landmarking feminist psychology as an academic and professional movement and in establishing the key category of "self-in-relation." The books Miller has coauthored with other women psychologists, including Judith Jordan, are *Women's Growth in Connection: Writings from the Stone Center* (New York: Guildford Press, 1991) and *Women's Growth in Connection: More Writings from the Stone Center* (New York: Guildford Press, 1994). Dorothy Dinnerstein, author of *The Mermaid and the Minotaur* (New York: Harper and Row, 1976), is among the most politically outspoken of the feminist psychologists. Her book calls for a more active role for fathers in childrearing. Nancy Chodorow, author of *The Reproduction of Mothering* (Los Angeles: University of California Press, 1978), works skillfully out of a Freudian revisionist and Object Relations perspective. Her pioneering work has provided the psychological basis for much feminist social theory. Also see her *Feminism and Psychoanalytic Theory* (New Haven, CT: Yale University Press, 1989) which broadens the perspective.

Carol Gilligan's *In A Different Voice: Psychological Theory and Women's Development* (Cambridge, MA: Harvard University Press, 1982) which blends sociology and psychology, is among the important groundbreaking books in women's studies. Catherine Keller's *From a Broken Web: Separation, Sexism, and Self* (Boston: Beacon Press, 1986) makes the key connection between the male ego and atomism; it is an invaluable survey. Ellyn Kaschak's *Engendered Lives: A New Psychology of Women's Experience* (New York: Basic Books, 1992) is an ambitious extension of theory into the social realm; it was among the most helpful and persuasively argued books I came across in my research. Betty Roszak's "The Human Continuum" in Betty Roszak and Theodore Roszak, eds., *Masculine/Feminine* (New York: Harper Torchbooks, 1969) is an early feminist analysis of gender psychology. Also see Betty

Roszak, "The Spirit of the Goddess" in Theodore Roszak, et al., eds., *Ecopsychology: Restoring the Earth, Healing the Mind* (San Francisco: Sierra Club Books, 1995) for an ecological extension of that analysis.

The violence to which troubled boys resort in their search to become manly men needs more study. Two books that offer insights are Dan Kindlon and Michael Thompson, *Raising Cain: Protecting the Emotional Life of Boys* (New York: Ballantine Books, 1999) and James Garbarino, *Lost Boys* (New York: Free Press, 1999).

Other important contributions to the discussion of gender, especially with regard to science and technology, include Judith Butler, *Gender Trouble: Feminism and the Subversion of Identity* (New York: Routledge, 1989) and *Bodies That Matter: On the Discursive Limits of "Sex"* (New York: Routledge, 1993); Timothy Kaufman-Osborn, *Creatures of Prometheus: Gender and the Politics of Technology* (Lanham, MD: Rowman and Littlefield, 1997); and Jean Barr, *Common Science: Women, Science and Knowledge* (Bloomington, IN: Indiana University Press, 1998).

Abraham Maslow's *Psychology of Science* (New York: Harper & Row, 1966) may be credited with opening the inquiry into the irrational dimension of modern science. Though he targeted the "tough-mindedness" and power-orientation of orthodox science, Maslow did not make questions of gender and feminism central to his critique. That approach owes as much to feminist historians and philosophers as to psychologists. These include Susan Griffin's *Woman and Nature: The Roaring Inside Her* (New York: Harper and Row, 1978), Carolyn Merchant's critical history of science, *The Death of Nature* (New York: Harper and Row, 1980), and her recent *Earthcare:*

Women and the Environment (New York: Routledge, 1995), and Evelyn Fox Keller's MacArthur Award-winning works *A Feeling for the Organism* (New York: W. H. Freeman, 1983), *Reflections on Gender and Science* (New Haven, CT: Yale University Press, 1985), and *Feminism and Science* (New York: Oxford University Press, 1996), the anthology she edited with Helen Longino. Mae-Wan Ho, *The Rainbow and the Worm* (London and Singapore: World Scientific Press, 1993), offers a searching methodological critique of reductionism in biology and suggests a noninvasive alternative. There are two important studies by Londa Schiebinger dealing with the historical background to gender bias in science: *The Mind Has No Sex? Women in the Origins of Modern Science* (Cambridge, MA: Harvard University Press, 1989) and *Nature's Body: Gender in the Making of Modern Science* (Boston: Beacon Press, 1993). Also see Mary Midgley, *The Ethical Primate* (New York: Routledge, 1994) and *Science as Salvation* (London: Routledge, 1992); and Stephen H. Kellert, *In the Wake of Chaos: Unpredictable Order in Dynamical Systems* (Chicago: University of Chicago Press, 1993), which suggests that there is a historical connection between feminism and Chaos Theory. Needless to say, all of Jane Goodall's books radiate the new scientific sensibility for which this essay appeals: *My Friends, The Wild Chimpanzees* (Washington: National Geographic Society, 1967), *Innocent Killers* (Boston: Houghton-Mifflin, 1971), *In the Shadow of Man* (Boston: Houghton-Mifflin, 1988), and *Visions of Caliban* (Boston: Houghton-Mifflin, 1993). For information about Jane Goodall's Roots and Shoots program for children, contact the Jane Goodall Institute, Box 14890, Silver Spring, MD 20911.

Critical insights into modern science can be found in Theodore Roszak, *Where The Wasteland Ends* (Garden City,

NJ: Doubleday and Co., 1972), *Person/Planet* (Garden City, NJ: Doubleday and Co., 1979), and *The Voice of the Earth: An Exploration of Ecopsychology* (New York: Simon & Schuster, 1992); Paul Shepard, *Nature and Madness* (San Francisco: Sierra Club Books, 1982); Morris Berman, *The Reenchantment of the World* (New York: Cornell University Press, 1981) and *Coming to Our Senses: Body and Spirit in the Hidden History of the West* (New York: Simon & Schuster, 1989); David Noble, *World Without Women: The Christian Clerical Culture of Modern Science* (New York: Alfred A. Knopf, 1992); and Brian Swimme and Thomas Berry, *The Universe Story* (San Francisco: HarperCollins, 1992). Charlene Spretnak, ed., *The Politics of Women's Spirituality* (New York: Anchor Books, 1982) and her *States of Grace: The Recovery of Meaning in the Postmodern Age* (San Francisco: HarperCollins, 1991) are persuasive feminist critiques of the latest stages in patriarchal philosophy, with special reference to science. Older works that raise searching questions about science and technology include Edwin A. Burtt's classic work, *The Metaphysical Foundations of Modern Science* (New York: Anchor Books, 1954), Lewis Mumford, *The Myth of the Machine* (New York: Harcourt, Brace, and World, 1967-70), and Seyyed Hossein Nasr, *The Encounter of Man and Nature* (London: George Allen and Unwin, 1968).

The best discussions of *Frankenstein* as a "feminist critique of science" appear in Anne Mellor, *Mary Shelley: Her Life, Her Fiction, Her Monsters* (New York: Routledge, 1988), and Brian Easlea's *Fathering the Unthinkable: Masculinity, Scientists, and the Nuclear Arms Race*, (London: Pluto Press, 1983), an incisive contribution to the gender bias underlying early science and the arms race. Roger Shattuck, *Forbidden Knowledge from*

Prometheus to Pornography (New York: St. Martin's Press, 1996) has an excellent chapter on Mary Shelley's treatment of the morally questionable edge of science. Jon Turney's *Frankenstein's Footsteps: Science, Genetics, and Popular Culture* (New Haven, CT: Yale University Press, 1998) reviews medical history and ethics within the Frankensteinian paradigm. *Screams of Reason: Mad Science and Modern Culture* (New York: W. W. Norton, 1998) by David Skal traces the Frankenstein motif through the movies.

The extraordinary contribution that women have made in the field of ethology, and especially in dealing with apes, has become a focus of study and controversy in feminist circles. Donna Haraway's *Primate Visions: Gender, Race and Nature in the World of Modern Science* (New York: Routledge, 1989) is the most ambitious as well as the most political analysis, spanning popular culture as well as science. Mary Ellen Morback, Allison Galloway, and Adrienne Zihlman, eds., *The Evolving Female* (Princeton: Princeton University Press, 1997) moves the discussion into the area of paleobiology. Also see Sy Montgomery, *Walking with the Great Apes* (Boston: Houghton-Mifflin, 1991), and Carol Adams and Josephine Donovan, eds., *Animals and Women* (Durham: Duke University Press, 1995).

The number of books dealing with new directions in science, especially studies in complexity, chaos, and new cosmology, grows by the day. An overview of the issues raised by these insights can be found in Theodore Roszak, "Nature and Nature's God: Modern Cosmology and the Rebirth of Natural Philosophy," *Michigan Quarterly Review*, Winter 1995. Among the more accessible studies of contemporary science that bear upon the thesis of this book are Louise Young, *The Unfinished Universe*(New York: Simon & Schuster, 1986); Lynn Margulis and Dorion Sagan, *Microcosmos: Four Billion Years of Microbial Evolution* (Berkeley: University of California Press, 1986); Menas Kafatos and Robert Nadeau, *The Conscious Universe* (New York: Springer-Verlag, 1990); Paul Davies and John Gribbin, *The Matter Myth* (New York: Viking, 1991); Paul Davies, *The Mind of God*, (New York: Simon & Schuster, 1992); Peter Coveney and Roger Highfield, *The Arrow of Time* (New York: Fawcett-Columbine, 1992); Hubert Reeves, *The Hour of Our Delight* (New York: W. H. Freeman, 1993); Fritjof Capra, *The Web of Life* (New York: Anchor Books, 1996); and Michael Behe, *Darwin's Black Box: The Biochemical Challenge to Evolution* (New York: Touchstone Books, 1996). On complexity studies, see Stuart Kauffman, *The Origins of Order* (New York: Oxford University Press, 1993) and *At Home in the Universe: The Search for Laws of Self-Organization and Complexity* (New York: Oxford University Press, 1995); M. Mitchell Waldrop, *Complexity: The Emerging Science at the Edge of Order and Chaos* (New York: Simon & Schuster, 1992); and George Johnson, *Fire in the Mind: Science, Faith, and the Search for Order* (New York: Alfred A. Knopf, 1995). Brian Goodwin's *How the Leopard Changed its Spots: The Evolution of Complexity* (New York: Touchstone Books, 1996) is an elegant and groundbreaking study of morphological tendencies in evolution that challenge standard Darwinian theory. Steven Rose's *Lifelines: Biology Beyond Determinism* (New York: Oxford University Press, 1998) is a moving and persuasive humanistic critique of ultra-Darwinism. Henning Genz, *Nothingness: The Science of Empty Space* (Reading, MA: Perseus Books, 1999), reveals that even the void that was once assumed to hold all the isolated atoms in the universe apart is crowded with subtle webs and networks.

Marjorie Hope Nicolson's *Mountain Gloom and Mountain Glory: The Development of the Aesthetics of the Infinite* (Ithaca NY: Cornell University Press, 1959) does an excellent job of tracing the modern fascination with mountains back to its aesthetic origins. Simon Schama's *Landscape and Memory* (New York: Alfred A. Knopf, 1995) includes an astute analysis of mountains as "vertical empires, cerebral chasms."

about the author

Theodore Roszak is Professor of History at California State University, Hayward. He is the author of numerous bestselling books, including *The Making of a Counterculture*, *Where the Wasteland Ends*, and *The Voice of the Earth*. A Guggenheim Fellowship recipient, he has twice been nominated for the National Book Award and twice earned Goldman Environmental Foundation grants. His novels include *The Memoirs of Elizabeth Frankenstein* which won the 1997 James Tiptree Award for "fiction that illuminates the meaning of gender in our time." He lives in Berkeley, California, with his wife, Betty.

CONARI PRESS, established in 1987, publishes books on topics ranging from psychology, spirituality, and women's history to sexuality, parenting, and personal growth. Our main goal is to publish quality books that will make a difference in people's lives—both how we feel about ourselves and how we relate to one another.

Our readers are our most important resource, and we value your input, suggestions, and ideas. We'd love to hear from you—after all, we are publishing books for you!

To request our latest book catalog or to be added to our mailing list, please contact:

CONARI PRESS
2550 Ninth Street, Suite 101
Berkeley, California 94710-2551
800-685-9595   510-649-7175
fax: 510-649-7190   e-mail: conari@conari.com
www.conari.com